INDIAN FOLK AND TRIBAL
PAINTINGS

ISBN: 978-81-7436-465-4

© Roli & Janssen/Roli Books 2008
Published in India by Roli Books
in arrangement with Roli & Jansen BV
M 75 Greater Kailash II (Market), New Delhi 110 048, India.
Phone: ++91-11-2921227, 29212782. Fax: ++91-1129217185
Email: info@roli.com Website: www.rolibooks.com

Editor: Priya Kapoor
Layout: Kapil Taragi
Production: Naresh Nigam, Kumar Raman

Printed and bound in Singapore

INDIAN FOLK AND TRIBAL PAINTINGS

CHARU SMITA GUPTA

Lustre Press
Roli Books

CONTENTS

THE BEGINNING

Painting is an exquisite expression of human thought, and nature is an eternal source of inspiration. Art, in the Indian context, perhaps emerged when homo sapiens placed a coloured dot on a mud surface. For the artists of ancient times, Mother Earth was an available surface to draw on, with the help of fingers, twigs or bone points – which is why we do not have any existing examples of floor drawings from earlier cultures, as they could not withstand the ravages of time.

Starting from the Mesolithic period (8000 years BP),[i] there is definite evidence of the artistic ability of people in the form of paintings and engravings in rock shelters in several parts of India, which is the earliest recorded expression of art.[ii] Post-Independence, there has been much focused research on rock art in India.

The origin of folk and tribal art forms had a direct co-relation with rock art,[iii] which showed a sequential development in the theme and character of drawings, according to the lifestyle of the group. The thought and expression of the hunter tribe of the Mesolithic period from 12000–6000 years BP was different from the painting of the Neolithic period from 6000–5000 years BP, the Chalcolithic period from 5000–2500 years BP, and the early Iron Age, 2500–300 years BP, where communities went from hunter-gatherer to pastoral and agricultural activities. This transition enabled them to have spare time for leisure activities. More developed rock

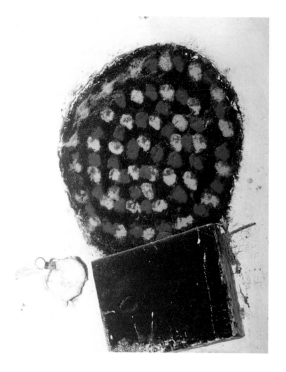

paintings, which emerged from early history (300 BP–AD 800), to the medieval ages (AD 800–1300), and more recent times (AD 300–till present)[iv] had secular, courtly or monastic themes. The paintings were created with bare hands, using fingers, thumbs, fists or palms, or with the help of twigs, bones or other brushes created with available indigenous material, and sharp cutting instruments were used to incise the images. Hammered strokes on a chisel placed on the rock surface also created lines and drawings. It is very interesting to note that iron oxide or haematite has an extensive range of shades from orange to dark brown and even purple. Therefore, shades of haematite along with white, green and black colours were the commonly used pigments on these rock paintings. The sources of white, green and black colours are not established, but manganese, natural earth, and charcoal, both natural and burnt, were used with animal marrow as a medium. Simple pulverization of the colour nodules in a water solution created the colour. This was then applied directly on an unprepared surface, perhaps after mixing the colour with natural adhesives.[v]

There were mainly two types of motifs which were drawn in the earliest recorded paintings. These were pictographs (the painted images) and petroglyphs (the incised images).

Today, there are about 1,500 rock-painting shelters at more than 150 sites in India.[vi] Some

of the rock shelters in central India had a long history of human habitation and offered rich material for experts. Archibald Carlleyle, an archaeological superintendent of the Archaeological Survey of India, first discovered rock paintings at Sohagighat near Mirzapur in Uttar Pradesh in 1860. In 1917, Percy Brown, an architect, described the drawings from Raigarh and Mirzapur as the most realistically rendered hunting scenes depicting a chase between wild animals, specifically a rhinoceros and a stag. Manoranjan Ghosh, an Indian archaeologist, explored and studied the rock paintings at Chakradharpur in Singhbhoom district in Orissa; Mirzapur in Uttar Pradesh; and Singanpur, Raigarh, and Hoshangabad

districts in Madhya Pradesh in 1932. V.S. Wakankar, a renowned archaeologist from India, explored and reported a large number of sites in 1973, while Yashodhar Mathpal, an archaeologist specializing in rock art, discovered several sites in Kerala at Tenmalai in Quilon district, Ancode in Trivandrum district, and Edakkalguha and Toberimala in Wynad district with petroglyphs and at Idukki and Palghat with pictographs.[vii]

Petroglyphs were discovered by the archaeologist F. Fawcett at the beginning of the twentieth century in the cave of Edakal in the Kozhikode district of Kerala.[viii] Paintings in the caves of Kerala were divided into seven phases, ranging from the beginning of the late

Left: Wall painting showing human, animal, and floral motifs, lime colour, Sawai Madhopur, Rajasthan.

Right: Santhal woman with tattoo marks on forehead and cheeks symbolizing Bhimal Pinnu, the rain god, Orissa.

Wall drawings in geometric patterns on the outer wall of a hut; Gadaba tribe, Orissa.

Mesolithic period (about 4000 years BP) to the late Megalithic period (about 1000 years BP).

Paintings of Phase I depicted animals in the wild, mainly deer, and were about 4,000 years old. Paintings of Phase II were linked to the Neolithic period, when the domestication of animals and plants began. A direct link between the domestication of animals was noticed in the paintings that have been bracketed around 3500 years BP. Paintings of Phases III, IV and V were dated to 2700, 2500 and 2200 years BP, and were associated with the Megalithic culture. The inhabitants of the sites of this period decorated the rocks with drawings. The paintings of the last phases, Phases VI and VII, date back to 1500 and 1000 years BP.

The paintings executed in white pigment illustrated hunting scenes – horse-riders, elephants and bull-riders – and geometric drawings – buds, tridents and other signs were also drawn. There was a very close similarity in the paintings of this phase to the contemporary practices of folk and tribal art. These paintings were found on the uppermost layers of the rock surface and looked very fresh.[ix] The white pigment was mostly prepared from limestone and sometimes from bird droppings.[x]

Several rock paintings from the earlier and later historical sites – pre-Neolithic and Neolithic – were from the Raichur, Bellary, Gulbarga and Bijapur districts of north Karnataka. Most of the rock paintings were in Tungabhadra in Gangavati, Hospet taluk, particularly in Hire Benkal in the Hampi area.

Paintings at Chik Rampur exhibited distinct similarities. Red ochre in three shades, that is, dark red – almost scarlet – brownish red, and bright red had been used in earlier paintings. Two colours, yellowish white and black, were used in some paintings, while those that used lime for white showed a very bright effect.

Ninety per cent of the rock shelters are in Madhya Pradesh, where the sandstone hills in the Vindhya, Mahadeo and Kaimur ranges are known to have formed rock shelters and caves. Banda, Bastar, Bhopal, Chamba, Chhindwara, Chhatarpur, Damoh, Datia, Gwalior, Hoshangabad, Jabalpur, Mandsaur, Morena, Narsimhapur, Nimar, Panna, Pachmarhi, Raigarh, Raisen, Rajgarh, Rewa, Sagar, Satna, Sehore, Shivpuri, Vidisha and Durg in Madhya Pradesh all boast of shining examples of rock painting in India.

The site at Bhimbetka in Madhya Pradesh is one of the oldest known sites in India. The seven hills in Bhimbetka in the western Vindhyas, about two kilometres southwest of the tribal hamlet of Bhiyanpur in the Raisen district of Madhya Pradesh, has over 600 rock shelters. Bhiyanpur is geographically forty-five kilometres southwest of Bhopal and thirty kilometres northwest of Hoshangabad. There were several hill tribes of Madhya Pradesh living in the small hamlets around the Bhimbetka hills and they specialized in tattoo designs and palm impressions on walls. However, Yashodhar Mathpal[xi] is of the opinion that Bhimbetka was perhaps the seat

Above: Rock painting showing elephant with rider.

Left: Rock painting showing Shiva.

Wall mural showing
a long carriage,
Shekhawati,
Rajasthan.

of Bhimsen or Bhim, one of the five Pandava brothers, the heroes of the epic Mahabharata. He was massive and had tremendous physical strength. A venerated hero in tribal mythology, he is recognized as a sky god among the Saora tribe of Orissa, a moon god by the Bondo tribe of Orissa and as Bhimal Pannu, the god of fertility and rain, by the Kond tribals of Orissa. The Gond and Baiga tribals of Madhya Pradesh honour Bhimsen, who is believed to have discovered the ardent spirits.[xii] He is also a hero for the Korku, the oldest tribe of central India, whereas the Muria, the tribals from Chhattisgarh, regard him as the inspiration behind roaring thunder. The carvings of the Korkus were found on stone pillars as early as the ninth or tenth century near Pachmarhi and Tamia.[xiii] It is possible that there may be a direct link between the Korku art of carving and the rock paintings of Bhimbetka.

The affinity between rock paintings and contemporary tribal art cannot be missed. Though today the colours are a mixture of natural materials and manmade shades, tribal art continues to be simple and direct. Tribal people have a strong awareness of their surroundings and this is reflected in contemporary images such as trains, aeroplanes and motorcars drawn with a hunter or a farmer on the same canvas. A similar awareness of surroundings was expressed in the paintings of Bhimbetka art. Before talking about contemporary folk and tribal art, it is thus important to describe briefly the rock shelters of the Bhimbetka region. These rock shelters can be divided into two groups:

1. Scenes of hunters and food-gatherers in five phases from the prehistoric period.

2. Riders on horses and elephants with metal weapons in three phases from the historic periods.

Single and dual colour paintings were executed in mineral colours, mainly white and red; however, the colour blue was never used. The paintings of the earlier phases starting from the Mesolithic period had common everyday themes, like father and son and other family depictions; profiles of women; hunting scenes with a forest full of animals like deer, buffaloes and mythical boars, fallen prey to hunters. Drawings of the earlier historic phases showed bands of soldiers marching or in battle, cavaliers and elephant-riders, royal processions and royal personages. Judging from their dress and weapons, the soldiers and cavaliers appear to belong to the Sunga and Kushana periods (first century BC to fourth century AD).

The paintings were executed in three styles – natural, geometric and abstract – and were silhouetted, decorative, partially filled or outlined. Some of the figures had what can be called, in contemporary parlance, an ultrasonic style, with depictions of the inner functions of the human body, for example, the womb and the foetus. Ganga Devi, a contemporary folk artist, has used this technique in her painting 'Life Cycle' where she has shown a pregnant woman with a view of the child inside her. This painting is currently in the collection of the National Handicrafts and Handlooms Museum, New Delhi. These cave paintings lacked the concept of a foreground or background for the human or animal figures that they depict – they were independent and complete in themselves. Shadows on the ground formed by the figures were conspicuously missing.

Jaya Appasamy[xiv] defines folk art by five distinctive characteristics:

1. Preference for simple outlines, choice of typically representational lines, and rejection of accessory elements.

2. A simplification of volume and colours, to eliminate shading.

3. Exaggeration of gestures for dramatic expression and primitive use of relative size.

4. Stylization of motifs to create decorative elements.

Portrayal of a family, shown with an aeroplane and bicycle, Shekhawati, Rajasthan.

5. The repetition of lines, entire figures and dots for intensive or rhythmical purposes.

There is a definite continuity in the character and style of the rock and cave paintings of prehistoric artists, and contemporary folk and tribal art. Artists derive their inspiration mainly from their surrounding environment, but the rendering of forms is often not a naturalistic depiction. Folk and tribal art creates a parallel reality, which is simple in character.

Art, among the tribal and folk communities in India, was never indulged in purely for pleasure. Its purpose was equally to pacify the malevolent deities and to pay homage and express gratitude to the benevolent ones.

Festivals are linked to the two agricultural crop cycles of sowing, reaping, harvesting, and storing; festivities are also related to events such as birth, puberty, marriage.

Kolam, a custom in south India entailing daily decoration of the mud floor, was considered essential to welcome the household deities. In the belief that paintings on walls and floors bring peace and harmony to the dwelling, the main doorway of the house, the inner quarters, the kitchen – all display painted details for protection of the household goddess and to ward off evil. Apart from colour, clay relief-work is also used for similar purposes. The Agaria and Gond communities of Madhya Pradesh, Harijans of Madhubani and many groups in north India, particularly girls in Haryana, work with clay. These clay relief decorations, known as *sanjhi*, may be termed as painted appliqués, with lumps of clay, either plain or mixed with rice husk and jute, and are customarily used as material for creating forms. The areas of the house considered to be auspicious are decorated with such clay relief forms by a group of women. Red ochre and lime colours are then added to these designs. Since collectiveness is a reflection of group solidarity, these reliefs are not done by a single woman but in collaboration by a group of women. This brings forth another characteristic of folk and tribal art – group cohesiveness, instead of art as an individualistic expression.

While travelling through the villages of Andhra Pradesh in the twenty-first century,

Facing page: Detail showing the foetus of a pregnant women as depicted by Ganga Devi, Madhubani painting.

Below: Lifecycle of women as depicted by Ganga Devi, Madhubani painting. This frame shows *shasti puja*, a ceremony on the sixth day after the birth of a child.

Right: Geometric paintings on the main doorway of a Mehar hut, Gujarat.

Below: Painted Ganesha riding on his mouse vehicle, wood, Maharashtra.

one comes across houses in places such as Pochampalli in Nalgonda district, which have cow dung smeared on the walls at the entrance, against a black background, along with five, seven, nine or more dots of turmeric and red ochre. The black background is created by smearing charcoal. Friday is the auspicious day, when the floor in front of the main door of all houses is smeared with fresh mud plaster decorated with the *muggu* pattern. *Muggu* (design of dots and lines) is the traditional floor decoration of Andhra Pradesh, made by the Padamsale, the weaver community of this region. Images of Bhavna Rishi and Markandeya are painted on the inner walls of their dwellings, but Yellamma, the female deity, does not have an iconic form. She is represented by dots in yellow and red using turmeric and red ochre. The houses may have well-plastered walls but the motif, which is mainly for protection from the evil eye, is painted in the conventional style. This definitely forms part of the magicoreligious practice, which perhaps was the genesis of tribal and folk paintings in prehistoric times. Similarly, *gauri* (the *samadhis* of the departed family members of the

Padamsale) have painted motifs on a white background. Painted cenotaphs are also seen in the Bastar region of Chhattisgarh.

As time progressed, scientific and technological advancements pushed magicoreligious practices into the background. But the presence of painted corners on whitewashed walls – a protection against the ill will of any visitor – clearly speaks of the fear of the supernatural. Although scientific developments have decreased the popularity of magicoreligious paintings, the art form still exists, but on a smaller scale.

Today, when one speaks of tribal and folk paintings in India, one has to look at the vertical as well as the horizontal spectrum. Historically, paintings created on rock surfaces by wandering communities were undoubtedly the first recorded expression of art. Art forms of the settled communities also appeared on the walls and floors of their dwellings. Vertically speaking, the art of painting expanded from floors and walls to other surfaces like clay, terracotta, stone, wood, ivory, glass, leather, palm-leaf, fabric, paper, papier-mâché and coconut, using one-, two- and three-

Left: *Mandana* painting, Sawai Madhopur, Rajasthan.

Right: Rajasthani woman outlining a *mandana* painting with lime paste on the floor.

Left: Painting on ivory showing Mughal emperor, Shahjahan.

Right: Astrological painting showing the *navagraha* (nine planets). From left to right are Budh, Shukra, Chandra, Guru, Surya, Mangal, Ketu, Shani, Rahu.

dimensional surfaces. There are ample examples of geometric drawings, comparable to the pictographs of rock art. Horizontally, regional- and community-based diversification of the styles of painting became distinct.

Wall and floor drawings continued to be an inherent part of everyday rituals and decorative art practices. Paintings led to the development of temple murals and fragments of these depictions appeared on wooden storytellers' boxes. Slowly, with technological advancements, the new materials became the additional surfaces on which to paint. Ivory, wood and stone were naturally available, but materials like fabric, paper, glass and papier-mâché were introduced as surfaces for painting in the later

periods. It is interesting to note that though contemporary folk and tribal paintings are similar in execution to the ancient rock art, the tribal and folk populations living in the vicinity of the rock shelters have not claimed any direct or indirect link to this ancient art form. Today, the study of rock art has shifted from a linear chronological approach to a diachronic interpretation.[xv]

Pupul Jayakar has categorized Indian tribal and folk paintings into several groups, according to the historical progress of these styles:

1. Rock paintings.
2. Pictographs on walls or pottery.
3. *Mandalas* (circular drawings depicting cosmic energy).

4. The magical or ritual drawings on doors and walls.

5. Ritual or festive narratives on walls.

6. Narratives on other surfaces like paper, cloth, palm-leaf, wood, glass, ivory and clay.

7. Astronomical and astrological paintings.[xvi]

Therefore, one can conclude, that once a beginning was made, as seen in the rock paintings, there was no turning back. In the forthcoming chapters, we are going to talk about the history of the styles and surfaces, the various manifestations of painted forms, and the identified folk and tribal paintings. The most important feature of this monograph is that the cluster of folk and tribal paintings is termed as the 'journey's merging and marching on'. The discussions here are centred on continuity, change, blends, and the emerging trends. The prime focus of folk and tribal paintings today is that most have made their mark as individual painted styles on the international scene. A large number of contemporary Indian folk and tribal paintings have thus found a place on the global map.

Jambavanta Purana scroll of the Madigas, a caste group of Andhra Pradesh, early 20th century.

STYLES AND SURFACES:
A BRIEF HISTORY

Many scholars have defined Mesolithic art as cultic art, in the sense that it was part of man's attempt to control nature and the environment through the rhythmic beating of drums, or dancing and singing loudly in circles. Human beings painted collectively, in order to banish fear, for ceremonial cures, or to express other cultic themes. The ecological environment in which people lived was hostile and human beings had not developed sufficient civilized technology to conquer nature. Man was skilfully portrayed as a meek creature pitted against the forces of nature in the rock paintings of this period. Motifs on rock paintings clearly relate to the flora and fauna, as well as human interaction with the surrounding environment.

Paintings from the Mesolithic period have often been labelled as 'archaic' or 'primitive', [i] but within the context of the period, they are nonetheless considered 'classic' and, as stated in the previous chapter, the earliest examples of the painted form. Aesthetic expression did not remain confined to a geometric repetition of forms but extended to the depiction of group activities such as hunting and dancing scenes. The lack of facial detail does not take away any value from these paintings in terms of the rhythm or action. The sketch of a baby deer in its mother's womb in a rock shelter at Bhimbetka in Madhya Pradesh, for example, is an imaginative and quite realistic expression of the intimate bond between mother and child, of one body and two lives. In a sense, such drawings were the forerunner of the ultrasound technology of today.

We may say that the rock paintings of the Mesolithic period were based on real-life experiences. The birth of a baby from the mother's womb confirmed its presence inside the mother's body, and this was illustrated in the paintings. Rock paintings in general did not focus on facial detail, which was perhaps not considered to be necessary by the artists. But rhythm, movement and action have been very well captured in them. We should not conclude by the available evidence that painters of that period did not draw any facial details. It is quite possible that in the paintings that were drawn for posterity on the upper parts of the rock – where they had a better chance of surviving the rigours of time – the emphasis was on actions rather than facial expressions. There may have been paintings drawn at the lower levels, which have not survived, where facial characters were drawn. There is a great deal of similarity in the rock paintings and pottery drawings of central India. There is also a very clear association between the rock art of the prehistoric period, and the paintings and pottery of the tribal communities in India.

India has a large tribal population, which forms about eight per cent of the total population of the country – the country perhaps has the largest number of tribal communities in the world. It is important here to understand the concept of the term 'tribe', which has been defined variously by different scholars. 'Tribe' has been defined as a self-contained society with a specific culture of its own, and confined absolutely to its own

Depiction of the origin of the Santhal tribe, Santhal painting, paper, early 20th century.

geographical boundary, living, as it were, in a world of isolation. The people of a particular tribe are bound by a common dialect, common resources for sustenance and belief in the same deities and traditions. Several indigenous groups have been declared as 'scheduled tribes', which are spread all over the country except Delhi, Haryana, Punjab and the two union territories of Chandigarh and Puducherry.

There are 427 tribes, including the subgroups as listed by the census records, distributed through the northeastern, eastern, northern, western, central and southern regions, and the Bay Islands zone.[ii] The eastern region comprises West Bengal, Bihar, Jharkhand and Orissa. The central region consists of the states of Chhattisgarh, Madhya Pradesh and Maharashtra, and has the maximum number of tribal communities – the Gonds, Bhils, Oraon, Saharias, and Warli. The western region comprises Rajasthan, Gujarat, Dadra and Nagar Haveli, Goa, and Daman and Diu. Some of the tribes of the eastern, central and western region – the Warli, Grasia, Bhil, Bhilala, Gond, Saora, Gadaba, Muria, Pradhan,[iii] Pando and Satnami tribes of Chhattisgarh[iv] – have made a distinctive mark in the art of painting.

In this chapter, we shall trace the history of tribal and folk art in brief, with reference to the surfaces and styles, which have emerged after, or in concurrence with rock paintings.

While elaborating on the history of folk and tribal art, we cannot ignore a large number of motifs, which appeared on pottery and seals

and were actually extensions of the pictographs and petroglyphs seen in rock art. Recorded evidence marks the presence of artistic practices from Neolithic times onwards in the northwestern part of the country and definite proof of settled societies has been found in parts of Punjab, Gujarat, Rajasthan, Haryana and Jammu and Kashmir. Excavations of Harappan art from 2500 BC revealed an exposition of new themes, most of which were encountered frequently in later periods. Numerous figurative and geometric designs seen in Harappan art continue to be executed even today, such as peacocks, peepul leaves and other floral designs,

tastefully painted in black over a red terracotta surface. A painted pot from Kalibangan, a Harappan site, shows a bird perched on a tree and at Daimabad, a post-Harappan site, a hemispherical bowl decorated with stylized animal and bird motifs, again in black on a dull red matt surface,^v has been found.

A terracotta vessel excavated from Lothal, belonging to the Harappan period, which is displayed in the National Museum, New Delhi, is an example of the developed geometrical motifs comprising a variety of cruciform, circular and rectangular shapes. Opposed triangles, two-headed axes, spirals, loops,

Bhil women sitting in front of a veranda's painted wall, Rajasthan.

labyrinths, chequerboard patterns, and tridents, also belong to the same period. These motifs were seen again in the folk depiction of Hindu gods and goddesses. Motifs such as the bow and arrow symbolically represent Rama, the incarnation of Vishnu, while circles and triangles represent female and male cosmic energies in tantric art. Inverted triangles placed one above the other, with their tips meeting in the centre, symbolically represent Shiva and Parvati in eternal union.[vi] Apart from the depiction of flora and fauna, the scorpion motif also appears frequently on the pots of earlier periods.

Female potters in present-day Kutch, Gujarat, paint similar motifs with white lime and black on red containers. A stick is dipped in colour and the motif is drawn on the pot while it is continuously rotated. In fact, seeing a contemporary potter woman at work takes us back in history to Chalcolithic times. Perhaps then, too, the men made the pots while the women decorated them. Decorative art on pots has not changed much down the ages. The women of Kutch have remained confined to black and white colours and geometric or animal motifs. There were also established traditions among the folk communities in Orissa, West Bengal, Uttar Pradesh, Madhya Pradesh and Tamil Nadu, using decorated pots to welcome the new harvest and to celebrate other auspicious occasions.

The first surface available to folk and tribal artists was the wall. At this point, there were two parallel developments. The settled

communities shifted to painting the walls of their abode, but these paintings have not survived because of the fragile nature of the materials used for construction of the huts. Paintings on mud walls were recorded later in history around the eighteenth century and are discussed later in this chapter. Wall paintings are called murals, and the term is generally extended to include paintings on ceilings, pillars and other architectural units.[vii] Generally, the paintings were not confined to one wall and a continuity of the theme flowed from one wall to another. The portrayals of scenes were usually inspired by the *Jataka* stories of the Buddhist tradition.

The earliest classical murals were from Ajanta, Badami, Bagh, and Sittannavasal.

Murals, both in houses and in early Buddhist monasteries, date from AD 200–700. The continuity of the Ajanta tradition was seen in the cave paintings of AD 600–900 and Badami paintings (AD 578), now ruined, were similar to the Ajanta drawings.[viii] The early Ajanta paintings (AD 200–500) were unique since a wealth of narrative detail was fitted into a confined space, while retaining an aesthetic appeal. The artists assigned to painting the walls of monasteries were master practitioners of mural art and the wall paintings of this period are a skilful depiction of the *Jataka* stories.

The Bagh cave paintings of Madhya Pradesh were also a continuum of the Ajanta style, but the Ajanta murals of AD 700 were not true frescoes because the colours were not bonded to the plaster on the wall by means of a thin coat of calcium carbonate. These are the best preserved examples of paintings on the cave walls. The lime base was perhaps derived from calcinated shells, laid over layers of a coarser mixture of straw, clay and powdered rock in a very thin and fine spread. The lime finish was then polished, which created an ivory-smooth, ready surface for painting. Mineral, earth, organic and alchemical pigments were used for painting.[ix] The colours were mixed with *gond*, the Indian gum, with a proportion of drying oil such as the juice of *neem* or *kapittha*. The technique of paintings was fresco, that is, colours applied on a wet surface and allowed to set. Body contours in these murals were drawn in light red and reinforced in black, and faces were usually shown in a three-quarter profile. The groups of dancers, musicians, saints, royal personages, soldiers and attendants, horse-riders, elephants, floral and geometric bands, all formed a part of the narratives depicted in the cave paintings.

This tradition of painting murals continued in medieval times in several kingdoms of south India as well as in Ellora in Maharashtra, Brihadisvara in Thanjavur, and the Virabhadra temple in Lepakshi, Andhra Pradesh. The Satavahana, Pallava, Pandya, Chalukya, Rashtrakuta and Hoysala kingdoms of the south depicted temple murals based on Hindu mythology, the epics, and the *Puranas*. During the period of the Vijayanagar empire, variety, grandeur, authentic familiarity of religious lore and the technical competence of the artist guilds was reflected on temple walls for

Facing page: Wall mural, Rajasthan.

Below: Detail of an Indian mural painting (depicting a musician playing for Lord Vishnu) in Mattancherry Palace, which was built by the Portuguese in 1557 and presented to the raja of Cochin.

appreciation by worshippers and visitors. The subject matter for temple murals was mostly drawn from the lives of common folk, who were the chief propitiators of these traditions. Female rotundity and a three-quarter profile of the face continued to be the main features of these frescoes. Contour lines boldly defined the outline and details of the body.

Mural paintings of Ajanta were generally narrations from the life of Buddha from birth to renunciation, whereas paintings in the temples depicted narratives, such as those from the *Bhagvata* and other *Puranas*. Murals of the later periods, from AD 1600 onwards, belong to Punjab, Himachal Pradesh, Rajasthan, Kerala and Tamil Nadu. Sacred wall paintings were found in the courtyards of temples in Nathdwara, Rajasthan. The Vishnu temple at Manapur, known as Chhati Kachahari, in the Lalitpur district of Uttar Pradesh, was built in AD 1130–1165 and depicted stories from the *Panchatantra*.[x]

The expressive style of the mural art of Kerala depicted the direct influence of the theatrical conventions of Kuttiyattam and Kathakali and has existed since AD 1000. Reaching an artistic peak during the seventeenth and eighteenth centuries,[xi] these are among the best frescoes of India. Gods, sages, kings and demons gave shape to the stories in these murals and the themes were inspired by epics and religion. Kerala has the second largest number of architecturally important mural sites – the palaces of Krishnapuram and Padmanabhapuram and the Ettumanur and Tiruvattar temples are among the best. It is a point of debate about whether these murals belong to the classical art form or the folk tradition, but the affinity of these paintings to contemporary folk theatre brought them closer to folk paintings.

The art of mural painting was just as constant and diverse as rock art. Regional styles also varied according to the period and place of execution.

It is quite possible that the common folk visualized these temple murals in paintings at

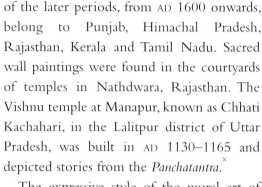

Facing page: *Pata chitra* showing *Kalia mardan*, Krishna killing the demon cobra; silk, Raghurajpur, Puri, Orissa.

Below: Radha-Krishna painting on paper.

the village level on walls, fabric, paper or wood, in their localized style. In the tradition of painted fabrics known as *kalamkari* in Telangana, *pat* in Andhra Pradesh, and *Mata ni Pachedi* in Gujarat, the influence of the temple mural art of earlier periods was clearly visible.

It is difficult to establish exactly when painting on mud walls of huts began. But, it has been an established tradition since the seventeenth century. Murals depicting religious themes were also found in the folk and tribal communities. The Osakothi ritual paintings of the Ganjam district of Orissa,[xii] the Rathwa[xiii] murals of south Gujarat, and the Dev Narayan murals of Rajasthan are typical examples of painted local shrines.

Apart from religious themes, murals were also secular in nature. The rural areas of eastern Gujarat, particularly the Anand and Khera districts, had a tradition of decorating the outer walls of their *havelis* (traditional houses). This was done to declare the social status of the affluent in the village society. Most of the houses belonged to the upper castes such as Amins, Patels and Brahmins.

The symbols used in the paintings usually consisted of the sun, the mythical animal, *sharabh*, the *gajasingha* (half-lion, half-tiger), stylized motifs of flowers, the *satadal* (the sacred motif of the lotus decorated with rays representing the cosmos), along with imagery such as men stopping a tiger from attacking the *satadal*. There is even a mural painting of an Englishman taking his pet for a walk, holding a walking stick in his hand. The motifs were sometimes extensions of religious beliefs associated with local deities or auspicious occasions and festivals and also showed the influence of invading cultures.[xiv] Secular themes, such as the social group's worldview, war, and hunting scenes, were also seen on the outer façades of palaces. These types of secular wall paintings are found in Amber, Bairat and Bhaopur in Rajasthan; and Sujanpur Tira in Himachal Pradesh.[xv]

Wood and paper became the preferred surfaces for illustrations with the emergence of manuscripts. Wood was first used as a surface for painting in AD 1000 in eastern India.[xvi] Bengal and Bihar evolved this technique during the Pala period, and the tradition then penetrated into Nepal and then on to Tibet. Manuscripts on wood have been found in Bengal, illustrated with Buddhist themes. The outlines were drawn in black or red, while the colours used were white, indigo, blue, red, yellow, black and green (green being a mixture of orpiment and indigo).

Illustrated manuscripts in the Jain tradition first appeared in AD 1300–1500. Although these paintings were executed for the Hindu courts, they resembled folk art.[xvii] The typical manifestation of human faces in profile in Jain miniatures gave them an affinity with folk art. Angular painting was the main characteristic of this style – the protrusion of the farther eye was emphasized, the nose and chin were pointed and the postures were formal,

Outer walls of a residential dwelling are the surfaces for painting in villages and towns. Such paintings, generally secular in nature, are visible from a distance.

Facing page: Details of a wall mural showing Lord Jagannath, Puri, Orissa.

Kuppi, gunpowder case, painting on wood and gourd, Rajasthan, early 20th century.

Facing page: Market scene, painted on a scroll, west India.

appearing stiff. The architectural details, although bold, were reduced to a minimum and there was no attempt at perspective, all the depicted actions occurring at the same plane. This style was very similar to the folk paintings on paper in later centuries.

Paintings on wood in the folk style were found in Thanjavur in Tamil Nadu, a continuous tradition since AD 1700. There are several examples of painted boxes in Andhra Pradesh, with illustrations that depict stories from the *Puranas* as well as from folklore. The tradition of narrative painted panels on folding doors was unique to Rajasthan – these wooden mobile shrines were known as *kavad*. A modern-day tradition of painting on wood is also found in the twenty-first century in Puri, Orissa. Here the Hindu gods, Jagannath, Subhadra and Balram, are shown as deep relief figures in the centre, and the single panels of the doors show episodes from Krishna's life.

Fabric must have been used as a surface for painting much earlier than the available evidence shows. In AD 700, Bana's *Harshacharita* referred to minstrels, who went around villages displaying painted scrolls describing the rewards and punishments exacted by Yama, the god of death.

Yama patas with similar themes are still painted by the scroll painters of present-day West Bengal. The *pataus*, as these painters are called, work on paper. But in AD 700, fabric was perhaps the surface for such scrolls.[xviii] The block-printed fabrics of Futstat, Egypt, dating

back to AD 900 confirm the decorative use of colours on fabric.[xix]

The earliest known evidence of paintings rendered on cotton fabric comes from Gujarat. These painted fabrics were made for trade with Sulawesi, eastern Indonesia in AD 1400. One such textile displayed a floral design with the leaf of the *sirih* plant known as '*daun bolu*' in Sulawesi, the fine design on the fabric not being block-printed but meticulously drawn by hand.

These painted fabrics from Gujarat were also used for rituals associated with house-building ceremonies, and at thanksgiving ceremonies celebrating a good harvest. These rituals were known as the *merek* ceremony. Red and blue were the two prominent colours in these paintings, the colour red being associated with life, strength and magical powers. It is difficult to say whether such painted motifs on fabric were meant only for trade, or also used as offerings by the local communities, but it was clearly established that there were painters who were painting on fabric for purposes of trade. The art of painting on fabric has existed as a continuous tradition in Gujarat, Andhra Pradesh and Tamil Nadu since the fourteenth century AD.

Most of the textiles meant for trade between Gujarat and the Indonesian market were block-printed. But a few rare examples like the one of the *sirih* plant mentioned earlier do exist, where the mordant and resist[xx] were applied with the help of a pen or country

From the seventeenth century onwards, the technique of painted textiles became very refined in the painted and mordant-resistant dyed fabrics of the Coromandel coast. The important motif that appeared in these painted fabrics, was the 'tree of life'. Repetitive floral motifs interspersed with birds and animals in fine brushwork were the characteristic feature of these painted fabrics. Ceremonial clothes with scenes from the Ramayana depicting bold human figures in indigo, yellow and red are other examples of the painted fabrics from the Coromandel coast in the late eighteenth century, which were exported to Indonesia. Noteworthy, is a unique textile piece which bore handwritten inscriptions on the surface, implying that it might have belonged to the Dutch East Indian company.

Going a little further in history, there were practising communities in Gujarat in western India and Andhra Pradesh and Tamil Nadu in south India, where hand-painted fabrics were used for ritual worship or as a part of the visual learning of the religious scriptures in temples. *Mata ni Pachedi* is the worshipped textile of Gujarat as *kalamkaris* are of the south. A detailed note on these painted traditions is presented in the chapter on lesser practices.

Scrolls were painted both for the Hindu aristocracy and for the village folk by the same painters. It is interesting to note that whether the paintings were for the market or for household customs, the continuity of the tradition came from regular practice and

brush before the textile was dyed. Another heirloom textile from Gujarat intended for trade with Sulawesi, dating back to 1500–50 AD, depicts a forest setting, with a prince and his consort in the centre surrounded by a series of female dancers and musicians. Larger-than-life depictions of the prince, his consort, and their attendants make the elephants and other animals appear diminutive. There is movement in each character, and the facial features bear a close similarity to the Jain manuscript paintings of the fifteenth and sixteenth centuries. The three-quarter facial profile and the protruding distant eye is characteristic of all the figures, except one or two, where the full profile is drawn. None of the figures have a complete frontal face.

sharing of skills between generations. Daughters learned to paint magicoreligious themes from their mothers, while sons learnt to paint for the market, as a source of income, from their fathers.

The painted and printed temple cloths, painted scrolls of the wandering bards and storytellers and the frescoes on temple walls served the same function of informally familiarizing the audience with religion and mythology. Painted cloths depicting Krishna with his *gopis* or cowherds were used as the backdrop for the Krishna icon, Shri Nathji at the Nathdwara temple in Rajasthan, an important centre of Vaishnav worship. Shri

Nathji appears at the centre of the painting, but his face does not show any distinctive features except for the massive silver lotus eyes to channelize the focus of the worshipper. A brilliant orange hue filled with the energy of exploding sunlight, forms the background of the paintings. *Picchvais*, as these painted backdrops are called, were adorned with the colours, flowers and ornaments of the seasons and the change of décor would be in harmony with the seasons. *Vasamalai*, the painted and printed cloths with mythological themes, were also an extension of the mural technique of narrating stories from the *Bhagvata* and other *Puranas*. These cloths are used to decorate

Above: Box for playing cards depicts Ganesha, the Hindu god, flanked by female attendants clad in the Maharashtrian-style sari, Sawantwadi, Maharashtra.

Left: *Phad* painting, Bhilwara, Rajasthan.

Facing page
Top: Painted tiger, wood.

Below: Jewellery box, painted wood, Rajasthan, mid-19th century.

temple walls and cover the wooden chariots that carry the *utsav murtis* (festive idols) in processions around the town for public viewing by devotees. *Vasamalai* were produced at Kalahasti, Nagapattam and Pallakolu in Andhra Pradesh.

In *Mata ni Pachedi*, the exploits of the seven Mother Goddesses are depicted.[xxi] These were painted and block-printed by artisans of the lower castes at the time of *navaratra*, the festival of nine nights celebrated after the rains, when the earth and the Mother Goddesses awaken. The archetypal form of the mother-figure riding a black male buffalo fills the centre of the cloth. Corn sprouts from the crown of the mother and surrounding her are her devotees, her son Ganesha, the *Bua*, her magician priest, the sun and the moon, horses and riders, dancing girls and milkmaids. The other manifestations of the goddess are: the four-armed Bahuchara, holding a sword, a spear, a bell and a cup of blood; Amba, the benign mother riding a camel; the sixteen-armed Bhadrakali, who rode a tame buffalo; Kalika, who used a cock as a vehicle, and Khodiyal, the lame mother who sat on a peacock throne. Chamunda rode a buffalo; Jogan, the ancient sorceress, strode forth, the sacral trefoil crown on her head. The cloths belonging to the deities were hung around the shrine and formed its roof. Apart from the main image of the different forms of the Mother Goddess, there are horizontal stripes running on either side, portraying episodes from the Ramayana and the *Puranas*. The two-headed golden deer hunted by Rama is one such portrayal.

The worship lasts for nine days. On the ninth day, Bua, the possessed priest, drinks fermented rice wine. He wraps the *pachedi* cloth of the goddess around his shoulder and leads a procession to the riverside, dancing and singing wildly. Unmarried girls carrying earthen pots, containing sprouted corn, on their heads follow him to the river bank, where they consign the sacral pot to the water as the culminating ritual in the worship of the departing mother. The main image in *Mata ni Pachedi* is block-printed, but the filler motifs and repetitive patterns are painted. The figures are again in profile. For a very long time, the painters working on these *pachedis* remained confined to the sacred uses of the paintings and did not explore the contemporary market for them. But now the younger painters are deviating from the strictures of the size of surfaces to be painted, and often paint smaller panels that have a wider appeal and can be sold commercially.

Paintings on other mediums such as paper have been recorded from the seventeenth century onwards. With the decline of the Mughal empire, the Mughal school of miniatures ceased to exist, and the artists moved to the independent states of Rajputana, the Punjab hills and Patna, in search of fresh patronage in the provincial courts. Under this patronage, at the end of the seventeenth and early eighteenth centuries, Indian miniature

Maler Mai, folk goddess detail of motif on *Mata ni Pachedi*, Gujarat.

Facing page:
Top: *Mata ni Pachedi*, painting on fabric, Gujarat.

Bottom: *Kalamkari* painting on fabric, Masulipatnam, Andhra Pradesh.

Folk miniature painting, showing Krishna with Radha, *gopis* and cows in the forest, Rajasthan.

Facing page:
Women flying paper kites, Kulu, Himachal Pradesh.

painting evolved its distinct features of jewel-like colours, smooth flowing lines, heavy-lidded, almond-eyed damsels with enormous nose-rings, and graceful stylized arrangements of trees and fountains. These schools of painting may be the earliest institutions of folk art. State patronage also gave birth to schools like the Kangra and the Pahari Kalam. In these paintings, nature was romanticized and inspiration was drawn from the scriptures. Rajasthan, in particular, gave birth to a plethora of folk art forms characterized by their fine format, strong colours and decorative designs. The Krishna Lila remained the favourite

subject of the Kishanganj and Kangra schools, which flourished in the eighteenth century. An interesting aspect of Kishanganj paintings was the portrayal of Krishna as an aristocrat instead of the cowherd playboy. Hunting and sports are also featured in the Kishanganj paintings.

Mewar and Malwa miniatures were characterized by their use of well-demarcated compartmentalized space. The influence of the Deccan was evident in the Mewar School of painting, where trees were often executed with paler green leaves over a prepared dark green surface. The themes ranged from sacred text to court scenes. Some of the descendants of Mughal painters, who migrated to Patna in Bihar around 1750–60, evolved fine, delicate, uniform paintings which got recognition as *Patna Qalam* around the mid-eighteenth century. These paintings were a mixture of the Mughal and European styles and may be grouped as the folk paintings of the eighteenth century.

At the same time, several manuscripts with folk illustrations were executed, which were not brought to the public or court's view. A large number of these manuscripts, are now being collected and documented by the National Manuscript Mission of the Department of Culture, Government of India, and should provide fresh testimony of painted folk art practices of different regions during this period. The documented data from these manuscripts are expected to bring volumes of information on the folk paintings executed on paper as well as fabric.

Pata chitra showing Krishna Lila; fabric, Raghurajpur, Orissa.

In Andhra Pradesh and Maharashtra, the tradition of wandering storytellers, known as *chitrakathis*, has long existed. Travelling from village to village, the *chitrakathis* bring the epics to life through mime and puppet shows, illustrating their recitations with paintings.

A series of paintings that have come to be known as Pratisthana paintings possibly represent the work of painters descended from artists at the court of the Vijayanagar kings. The illustrations are worked on thick ivory coloured handmade paper, and illustrate local variations of the Ramayana, the Mahabharata and legends from the *Puranas*.

The Pratisthana paintings of the eighteenth and nineteenth centuries were martial in mood and represented a strong male-dominated culture. There were scenes of battle, the hunting of savage beasts, and the destruction of malevolent female tree spirits and demons. The male heroes were symbols of the Vira Rasa, the heroic mood. Resplendent with bows and arrows, they were dressed in tightly tied *dhotis* and long flowing upper cloths or tight-fitted coats. The women appeared in subordinate roles, wearing tight bodices and flowing skirts, at times with their heads draped.

The Pratisthana painters use primary colours, mainly red, blue and yellow. The faces are drawn in profile; the features are sharp and the noses pointed. As in all rural paintings, the eyes are depicted in a frontal position, although the face is in profile. The colours are mainly used on the outlined bodies of humans and animals, while the background is a natural colour wash.[xxii]

There were several scholars in nineteenth-century India, particularly anthropologists and folklorists, who did not think it necessary to study or throw light on the paintings and other forms of art in inaccessible terrain. As a matter of fact, these scholars disassociated themselves from art produced in regions that were unapproachable and hence little known. The focus of these experts was on the study of political and social systems. Paintings which had a continuous existence in villages and centres of pilgrimage were termed 'primitive' by British connoisseurs of art. The concept of ethno-archaeology was non-existent. As in other traditions, so also in folk and tribal art, there is a continuity between the great traditions and the 'little' ones. When these art forms were brought to the notice of a wider audience, a great continuity was noticed in the ideology, thought and in many instances, even the form. The lesser or 'little' traditions of paintings had a continuous but unobserved existence in isolated small pockets. Written literature on folk paintings was not available until the twentieth century.

It was in the early twentieth century that Indian painting first came to be appreciated. Earlier, British scholars and art lovers paid attention only to Mughal paintings, but Ananda Coomaraswamy brought Rajasthani and Pahari paintings to a respectable forum, and paintings from other provincial courts followed suit. Coomaraswamy, as a scholar and an art critic, firmly added a fresh nuance to the aesthetic evaluation of all forms of Indian art and a beginning was thus made in the search for pictorial expressions of rural folk and tribal painters in a systematic way.

Folk painting from Bengal was the first to be recognized at the international forum, when in 1896 E.B. Havell became the head of the Calcutta Art School. He appointed Abanindranath, nephew of the great Rabindranath Tagore, as the vice-principal of Calcutta Art School in 1905.[xxiii] At this juncture Ajit Ghose, the collector and art critic, and Mukul Dey, the artist, exposed the Kalighat paintings of the areas surrounding the Kali temple in Calcutta. Ajit Ghose was eloquent in his praise of the archaic simplicity, largeness of style, and amazing boldness of the Kalighat paintings.[xxiv]

Around the same time, Guru Saday Dutt, an Indian civil servant of Bengali origin, acquired a large collection of paintings from rural Bengal. These paintings, termed as 'popular painting' by W.G. Archer, are now housed in the Guru Saday Dutt Museum in Calcutta. These vibrant works of art found respect and acclaim in international art circles and, for the first time, folk paintings were recognized outside their conventional setting. After Independence, with the abolition of the princely states, large collections of miniatures from provincial courts made their way to the market for sale.

Since the mid-twentieth century, India as a democracy has undergone rapid socio-cultural changes. These changes have taken place largely on account of India's effort to become

Tsunami, as depicted by Kalighat painter, West Bengal.

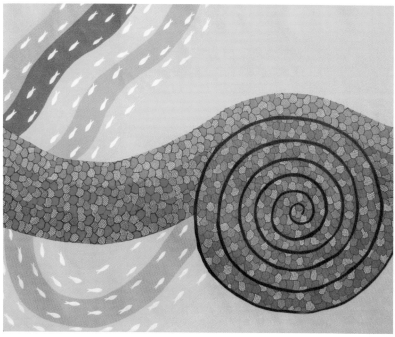

a global power in a short span of time. Alongside the strides that India has been making in the international arena, there has been a consistent effort to preserve handicrafts. Paintings from tribal or folk communities are recognized as proof of valuable hand skills. Much of the credit for bringing tribal and folk paintings out of the floors and walls of village homes, into cities and towns not only in India, but around the world, goes to promoters of handicrafts like Kamaladevi Chattopadhyay, Pupul Jayakar and Bhaskar Kulkarni.

To suit the demands of urban markets, the massive *kalamkaris* were reduced in size, curtailing themes while retaining the style. For instance, instead of a complete scene from the *Shiva Purana* only a small panel of Shiva and his consort would be drawn in the *kalamkari* style. The canvas was either reduced in size or changed from a wall to paper for some of the tribal and folk paintings, such as the Warli wall paintings of Maharashtra and Madhubani paintings of Bihar. Exponents of other styles such as Pithoro of Gujarat and Madhya Pradesh, Gond painting of Madhya Pradesh and *mandana* of Rajasthan, and many more, followed suit. This effort gave a new lease of life to the painters and the paintings.

The main purpose behind this impetus was to provide a life of dignity for the folk and tribal artists. As their canvas changed from walls and floors to paper and fabric, their paintings achieved a much wider visibility, and their skills came to be appreciated and rewarded by a growing audience, instead of remaining confined to the domestic sphere. Initially, the painters tried to rein in their imaginations, picking up motifs and designs from the traditional paint vocabulary and 'refitting' them to suit an urban audience. The main characters and content of the drawings thus remained unaltered in essence. But with exposure to new places and markets, the worldview of the painters began to change. Slowly, they began to synchronize their new vision with the traditional motifs on fabric and paper.

Folk and tribal art was till then considered a 'backstage' activity by art critics, who placed other art forms on a much higher pedestal. Folk and tribal art was never displayed in art galleries frequented by the media and the art collectors – it was only when tribal and folk painters began to be recognized at exhibitions

and in the urban market that art connoisseurs and critics began to give them attention. Finally, tribal and folk artists began to get the appreciation that was their due and national awards began to come their way. Among the folk and tribal painters thus honoured were Sita Devi, Jagdamba Devi and Ganga Devi in Madhubani, and Jivya Soma Mase for Warli paintings. Now, even the media, which had ignored them earlier, began to shower attention on these painters.

Cultural exchanges through the Festivals of India organized in the United Kingdom in the early 1980s gave another impetus to tribal and folk paintings. During one of these festivals, an exhibition entitled 'Aditi', a thematic depiction of the human lifecycle from birth to death, was organized. The panels made of papier mâché depicted marriage

Above: Women drawing *mandana* on the floor, Rajasthan.

Left: A Jogi woman painting, Gujarat.

Facing page: Paintings by Venkat Raman, a Gond tribal, using simple expansions of dots and lines in different shapes and colours to form images reflecting the tribal worldview.

scenes created by Chandrakala Devi, a folk artist from Madhubani, Bihar.

Traditionally, in Darbhanga district, women made small containers known as *changeri,* *pathiya,* or *dala,* by mixing paper and clay. They were painted with traditional, simple floral motifs and carried as gifts to the bridegroom's house during weddings. Several doll forms such as *kaniya* (woman with veil), *putariya* (maiden), *ma aur bachcha* (mother and child) were also made and decorated with colours. But for exhibitions, these Madhubani paintings were done on papier mâché panels instead of pots and doll forms.

The Warli painter, Jivya Soma Mase, was awarded the National Award by the All India Handicrafts Board in 1976 for a painting that depicts the tribal worldview and scenes from Warli tribal life, showing a *palaghat* deity in a square as the central motif. Village activities, dancing groups, animals and trees, cover the total canvas. Interestingly, the colours red, yellow and blue are used along with white, showing that these efforts were the beginning of individualism and creativity in tribal and folk art forms.

This exposure gave tremendous scope and vital energies to the painters who were encouraged to start being more imaginative in their paintings, using traditional themes as the base but matched to the taste of the buyer. Initially, the paintings were sold as wall canvases, where only one section of the narrative on a wall was selected or several isolated motifs were placed as a painting. This opened new gates for tribal and folk paintings, which emerged from their earlier isolation to take their place alongside other art forms in galleries and in people's homes far away from villages and rural areas of their origin.

The earlier constraints of surface and size which had come in the way of the commercial sale of folk and tribal paintings had been overcome once the painters were able to adapt to market demands. Painted styles such as those found in the bridal chambers of

Madhubani in Bihar, Warli in Maharashtra, and Bastar in Madhya Pradesh were noticed more and more for their artistic loudness and vibrancy. Laudable efforts by Pupul Jayakar and Bhaskar Kulkarni opened a new chapter in the history of tribal and folk paintings – Bhaskar Kulkarni provided paper to men and women in the Thane district of Maharashtra, the area inhabited by Warli tribals, and Pupul Jayakar made a similar effort in various villages of the Madhubani district in Bihar. The idea was to provide women with light labour in the famine-struck area.

However, when Jayakar visited Madhubani

Warli painting showing a tribal dance, paper, Warli, Maharashtra.

in the mid-1950s, she did not see paintings in the *gosain ghar* (the abode of the household deity) or the *kohbar ghar*, (the part of the home associated with marriage, fertility and childbirth), although W.G. Archer had earlier noticed such paintings in Brahmin and Kayastha homes. But Jayakar was confident of the natural artistic abilities of the women of the region. Young girls often practised on paper to learn how to draw auspicious motifs and symbolic decorations of both floor and wall paintings before they were allowed to actually participate in the specialized activity of drawing on walls or floors.

Back in the 1960s, women were not familiar with the brush or watercolours and used bamboo twigs and rags to draw and paint. Re-drawing motifs and drawings on paper, which were earlier drawn on the wall or floor, required some conceptual articulation according to the paper size. The results of the efforts made by Jayakar were visible within five months. Women's emancipation was evident in the poise and self-confidence of Mithila artists and Jitwarpur, Ranthi and Rashidpur were villages which came to be recognized on the international art map because of their women artists. Tantric paintings drawn by Brahmin *sadhus* were also brought to paper. A similar success story is that of the Warli paintings. Here, the magician priest made drawings on the inner wall space while women were allowed to draw and use colours on the outer walls. Warli men got

more recognition largely due to the efforts of Jivya Soma Mase, who painted his own worldview on a large canvas, stretching his imagination beyond the repetitive drawing of Kansari, the corn goddess. His acclaim was followed by recognition of the Gond and Bhil paintings, whch are discussed in detail in the section on popular paintings.

Another page was turned in the history of tribal and folk paintings. Exposure and display of the works of tribal and folk artists as individual practitioners of art gave rise to the need for more space for these art forms. They were more often written about and individual artists were recognized. Most importantly, art lovers felt a sense of pride in buying these works of art and displaying them for the world to see.

During the late 1970s and 1980s, the exploration for such art works in the interior villages of several states increased. Madhya Pradesh, Gujarat, Rajasthan, Andhra Pradesh, West Bengal, Maharashtra, Haryana, Tamil Nadu, Uttaranchal and Orissa emerged as the states where great volumes of art were brought to public view. While travelling by train, explorers searching for these indigenous styles could not miss the rows of hutments displaying white geometrical drawings in the distant view in Madhya Pradesh, or glimpses of colourful, eye-catching wall paintings amidst clusters of vegetation between Bhopal and Raisen. These were the secular paintings created at the time of the Diwali festival. The morphology of the paintings and the technique were different.

Rajwar women of Sarguja in Madhya Pradesh made architectural spaces such as verandas and niches their own, and painted them. Here and there a few animal, human or bird forms were also created and painted. These were three-dimensional paintings on a mixture of clay, rice husk and jute. Similarly, the Gadaba tribe in the Ganjam district of Orissa painted the outer and inner walls of their homes with broad bands of red, yellow, ochre and lamp black.

At times, bold yet simple flowers were also painted to adorn the inner walls. Despite international recognition, these art forms could not be brought to a wider market because there were few practitioners. Among the folk communities, the recognized caste groups of painters such as *chitrakar* or *nakkash* also brought their paintings for sale in the contemporary market. Scroll lengths were reduced and frames of episodes on scrolls or narratives were cut into sections so that these could be appreciated by the buyers and displayed in contemporary settings. But these groups of painters did not break away from their traditional psyche in terms of conventional themes whereas Ganga Devi, the Madhubani artist, Jangad Singh Shyam, the Gond painter and Jivya Soma Mase, the Warli artist, broke open the shell of traditional thought and moved ahead to paint what they saw and experienced with their exposure to a larger world. As their view of the

world expanded, they did not alter the technique or the colours, although sometimes the tools used to draw or paint were changed. Ganga Devi who was earlier using a reed *kalam*, switched over to an ink pen and later several artists started using a Luxor pen. But their lines, dots or the fillings remained distinct from the archaic past. This was the transformation without change. For example, an artist like Ganga Devi could paint a rollercoaster seen in the USA during her visits there for the Festivals of India, and still paint the *kohbar ghar* or portray traditional themes with equal ease. These artists started to paint what they saw in the modern world in their traditional styles and techniques. The contemporary artists did not influence them, but there were many artists trained in formal art schools who would look up to folk and tribal art for inspiration.

Another journey of the tribal paintings evolved when tribals like the Muria of Bastar in Chhattisgarh began to paint their images on paper instead of wood. Similarly, they started to depict dances and other activities of young men and women on paper. In the same vein, Santokhba Behn of Gujarat painted a large Mahabharata scroll solely through inspiration, displaying individual genius. These, then, are some of the emerging trends of the painted arts of folk and tribal communities.

Painted fabric, Masulipatnam, Andhra Pradesh.

Facing page: *Kavad*, painted wood shrine showing narratives from the *Bhagvata Purana*, Rajasthan, late 20th century.

MANIFESTATIONS OF PAINTED FORMS

When we deal with tribal and folk art, we are dealing with the art of people who are among us, who form a sizeable part of our population, living within the same ecological territories. An irregular stroke of brush or stick, firmness of style, uneven, non-rhythmic, rhythmic or repetitive forms are not deformities but the distinctive traits of tribal and folk art. Thought, surface, tools and pigments are four characteristic features of any painting. In this chapter we discuss briefly these four dimensions of painted forms.

Thought may be related to a sequence of themes or it may be an individual manifestation. Thought is depicted on a surface with the help of tools and pigments, as a collective expression of a group or an individual's expression. Collective thought, which is generally a group expression, has repetitive sequences of themes done by members of a particular community for a specific occasion.

There is clear intimacy between thought, folklore and culture. Generally, folk and tribal paintings have their origin in folk practices, which are an important aspect of folklore. Going into the literary meaning of folklore, we identify folk and lore as two distinct aspects. The term 'folk' applies to a specific community, whether tribal or non-tribal, while 'lore' specifies collective knowledge or wisdom on a particular subject. Lore is also often associated with myth, which is an important mode of human communication, teaching, knowledge and learning. There are several composite animal motifs, which are often used in Indian folk art. The *kinnara* (half-human, half-horse), the *gaja-simha* (half-elephant, half-lion), the *gaja-mina* (half-elephant, half-fish), the *kesari-*

Detail of *sharabh*, a mythical animal, on a *ganjifa* playing card.

Facing page:
Ganjifa playing cards, circular cards on paper, Orissa; rectangular cards; paper, Mysore, Karnataka.

simha (the tiger with a human face) and the *sona no hans* (the golden swan with the head and beak of the royal swan and body of a spotted deer), are examples of such figures. These mythical animals are often found in the folk art of Gujarat and Saurashtra. The *nabagunjara*, who has a head in the form of Krishna or a peacock, a foreleg in the form of a human hand, and a body which is a strange amalgam of the bull, the camel and the tiger, is often painted on *ganjifa* cards in Orissa.[i]

Since folklore is intimately associated with culture, we have to first look at this important aspect. It has been stipulated by scholars that folklore mainly depends on oral traditions and there is little margin for their re-creation or change in a developing society. However, when we look at the developing societies of today, we observe that although the basic genesis of folklore may not metamorphize, its manifestation and interpretations may see perceptible or imperceptible changes. Folklore encompasses the customs, knowledge systems, games, beliefs, practices, literature, performing and non-performing arts, which include dance, music, theatre, drama, painting, sculpture, making of crafts with several materials, festivals, and so on. The process of transmission of knowledge contained in all the aspects of folklore through sustenance, reshaping, renewal, and creation of variants has been a continuous phenomenon since human civilization appeared on this earth. Transmission of folklore is a time-sustained process.[ii]

Folk non-performing arts include painting, sculpture, objects made out of a variety of materials and body ornamentation through painting or tattooing. Painting as the sustained aspect of folklore has undergone several perceptible changes in folk and tribal cultures. There is a marginal or minimal difference between folk art and folk craft forms. Generally, the two-dimensional depiction of a myth is termed as a folk art form, while a three-dimensional depiction is categorized as folk craft. Manifestation of a myth may be both through a painting—which is a two-dimensional form — or any material such as clay, metal and glass, to give a three-dimensional form. Sometimes, ritualistic practices associated with a particular myth may also be simultaneously depicted in the painted or two-dimensional form, and a three-dimensional form. Occasionally, paintings are also done on three-dimensional surfaces such as a terracotta pitcher, coconut or conch shell. The tribal and folk painters generally adhere to the local techniques, traditions and themes and use local resources, including raw materials.

'Folk' generally means ordinary and non-literate people like villagers, labourers and tribal people from backward communities. Until recently, 'folk' also related to the primitive. Today, when we discuss folklore with reference to the development and dynamism of society, it needs to be re-designated. Folklore travels from one place to another with a group of people who have a

Painted lines on the forehead and arms depict the religious cult of this tribal.

Facing page:
Tattooing is the traditional body decoration. Here, a Toda tribal woman shows her tattooed arm, Tamil Nadu.

common cultural identity. The social identity of each group by way of life, language, tradition, and livelihood is patterned in a clearly identifiable manner. In the wake of large migrations from remote villages, whether tribal or non-tribal, to the urban metropolises like Delhi, Mumbai, Chennai, Kolkata and Bangalore, small pockets of indigenous cultural groups are created. They then become the adopted homelands of people who have migrated from a particular geographical area and share the same language, culture, mechanism of livelihood and living conditions. Their way of life and traditional heritage are bound by a common identity. These groups, even in the urban metropolises, express their folklore traditions through manifested verbal art, rituals, paintings and other art forms. However, their art and culture soon acquires a more sophisticated style of expression, in response to the demands of the city. Many tribal and folk painters, who have moved to the city, have found employment in government and private sectors. They are quick to see the selling potential of the painted art forms existing in the villages from where they have come. It is through the migrant folk and tribal people that these art forms have been popularized in the cities. Many painters from Madhubani in Bihar, for instance, are now settled in towns and urban metropolises in different parts of the country where their husbands or fathers have found employment.

Symbolic communication has been one of the important criteria for these paintings. Whether on the outer wall of a house or a temple or in the inner parts of a dwelling or place of worship, there has been an underlying purpose of symbolic communication. William Harmon has defined symbolism as 'an aspect of thinking expression in which the process of association is brought into play so that a concept or more often, a climate of thought is encompassed or suggested by a word, phrase, sign, gesture, object depiction of a diagram, etc.' [iii] That which is called symbolic, essentially invokes or arouses an association that conveys a particular meaning.

Symbolism in folklore is a recognizable and usable property of a cultural group. A symbol depicts the identity. A meaning is established with the identity and the purpose of communication is served. Symbolism in art acts as a standardized or stylized expression of various concepts, by which these symbols crystallize into a set shape or instantly recognizable form, as when the symbol of the sun is depicted as a circle with a face and a ring of stylized flames. The meaning expressed through symbols may range from small matter-of-fact, everyday details to concepts of cosmic importance, such as the gods and the spirit world. One may note in general, the prominence of symbolism connected with fertility, creation, and natural phenomena in tribal and folk cultures.

The forces of supernatural powers are also depicted with the symbol, which is a way of

Top: Bhil women.

Bottom: Pithoro painting showing details of a procession, Chota Udaipur, Gujarat.

Facing page: Kathakali dancer in the traditional costume.

appeasing these powers. Iconic and non-iconic forms and rituals are designed to accompany worship. Thus, the symbols in painted forms arise inevitably as a means of communication.

Thoughts are expressed through painting within specified practices by the recognized group of practitioners. Therefore, depictions of art forms in the folk and tribal traditions have continued to be an important means of learning about and understanding traditional myths.

PRACTICES AND PRACTITIONERS

The root of a particular thought or a concept may be similar in tribal, folk or traditional paintings. But it is the manner or form of depiction, which distinguishes one particular painted form from another. The manifestation of a particular thought, along with its development in a particular direction, determines a particular style of the painted art

Above: Household deity room with painted walls, Uttar Pradesh.

Right: Painted clay relief, Sona Bai Rajwar, Sarguja, Madhya Pradesh.

form. Folk communities, who have for long been in direct contact with the urban cultures, have more sophisticated forms of expression than those who have remained in the village or forest.

The paintings may be sacred or secular in character. There are several examples of sacred wall paintings in the inner spaces of the home, where the family deities are placed or where certain rituals are performed on festive occasions. Folk communities all over the country and a few among the tribal communities are associated with such wall paintings. The artistic ability to draw and decorate may vary from individual to individual but knowledge and execution of such paintings continues to be an essential part of women's socialization. There are several tribal wall paintings to satisfy the vanity of an unseen vital power, which is responsible for death, disease, fertility and other aspects of life. For example, it was a common practice of the Dangi tribes of the Dang district of Gujarat to display painted tigers on the outer walls of their dwellings. These tigers depict Vagh-dev, the tiger god, who is supposed to be very easily displeased and if angered, lifts cattle or hurts members of the family.[iv]

Domestic ritual art is an essential aspect of various celebrations from birth to death. The Indian tradition of floor drawings is known by various names in different parts of the country, such as *alopana*, *alpana* (West Bengal), *aipan*, *aripan* in Bihar, *sathiya* in Gujarat, *kolam* in Kerala, *mandana* in Rajasthan, *bhoomishobha*, *rangoli* in Maharashtra, and *apna* in Uttarakhand. In Uttar Pradesh, they are known as *chowk purana*, *sona rakhana*, *chitna*, *thapna*, *dharna*, *bharna*, *kadna*, *likhana*, *khodana*, and *jamana*. The terminology of these drawings is based on the kind of work involved. Most of them are done in innovative designs, weaving an exquisitely colourful filigree of patterns and colours.

These drawings are an everyday activity in some parts of the country and sometimes an occasional activity. The *alpana*, *kolam* and *muggu*, as some of these art forms are called, are walked over by family and friends during the day and become blurred. Each day, when the house is cleaned, a new drawing is created on the doorstep. At other times, the drawings are executed in order to communicate or announce specific occasions within the household, such as conception of a child, birth, puberty, adulthood, a boy's investiture with the sacred thread, and marriage. Some paintings are drawn as an act of wish fulfilment and may be termed as votive drawings.

In north India, rituals for a death in the family include drawing an image of the dead person with flour, on a floor plastered with cow dung, after the person has been cremated. These drawings are not walked over but are carefully guarded by a lighted lamp round the clock. The ceremony is completed by scattering grain on the image. It is a common belief that if a person meets an untimely death, the spirit of the dead person haunts the house to

Painted doorway, Rajasthan.

Thangka, with painting of Buddhist deity, Avalokiteshwara, Ladakh.

designs are common in both sacred and secular wall paintings, but the symbolic communication, magicoreligious importance and socio-economic significance of the two types may be entirely different or may have a marginal correlation. The motifs may be similar in both forms of painting, but the placement of a specific motif in a particular context makes it sacred or secular. Wall paintings are of central importance in tribal and folk art. The paintings of the Gadaba tribe of Orissa, Madhubani paintings of the Brahmin, Kayastha and Harijan communities of Darbhanga district in north Bihar, Bar Boond paintings of Kumaon in Uttaranchal, and the paintings of the Warli tribe in the Thane district of Maharashtra are a few examples.

Tribal and folk floor and wall paintings are diametrically different from traditional Indian art. The horizontal spread of the painting on the floor has been popularly called floor drawing mainly because the colours are used free-hand to make the geometrical patterns. Almost till half a century ago, the art of drawing on the floor was considered to be an essential skill for a young girl and would help her to find a good matrimonial alliance. Skill in drawing was considered a major attribute that would help her in managing her household responsibilities. Though there was a certain repetitiveness in the designs and patterns passed on from generation to generation, at times the learner was allowed to be inventive. The skills of drawing, handed down from mother to

torment the surviving relatives. The drawings on the floor are thus meant to keep the haunting spirits away from the site and prevent any harm to the living relatives. Similarly, paintings of *harkhi*, an evil spirit which spreads epidemics, or *churchesi*, a witch, are executed in red and black on the outer walls of the house on various occasions,[v] particularly when a child is born.

The techniques employed for both sacred and secular paintings are the same. Animal and floral motifs, human figures and geometric daughter, constituted a mark of achievement for each succeeding generation. Young girls usually started to draw at the age of about ten years and learnt to draw with a mature hand by their fourteenth or sixteenth year.

The material traditionally used in these diagrams is rice powder, which supposedly possesses magical power, and it is believed that this can scare away the evil spirits. An invoked presence finds its allotted place within the confines of the more or less intricate geometry of the diagram. Its malevolent power is said to be confined to the outlined space and thereby held in its place. Many of the drawings are without an image, figure, or narrative but have consistent and continuous geometry. The visual effect of these symbolic shapes is at one with their efficacy.

The geometrical designs lent themselves to being copied or adjusted to different techniques. When working on the floor, the artist has a direct contact with the surface to be painted and no brush or tool of any kind intervenes between the hand of the artist and the ground onto which the rice paste flows from the fingers. A small cloth soaked in this liquid medium is held in the right hand and when squeezed, allows the pigment to flow from the fingers in a steady, thin flux. This immediate contact of finger, paint and ground allows the direct translation from the artist's inner vision and experience into a distinctive non-figurative form. The imageless tracings on the floor display a different creative activity

visible from the process of representation and narrative in figurative art.[vi]

The figurative wall paintings are different from the non-figurative ritual drawings in other ways too. Colourful and rich in symbols, they are replete with mythical content. These wall paintings glorify a wall space, where household shrines are located or a room is decorated and made auspicious for the nuptial rites. There are a variety of forms created by the individual artists, but each of the artists is bound by the confines of the theme of the specific wall painting. For example, a wall painting created on the occasion of 'Ahoi Ashtami', the fasting festival for the well-being of sons, have specific drawings of 'Ahoi Mata', the mother, who is indicated by hands and feet on a triangular body, sometimes with the head missing or as a complete woman standing in the centre. The other decorations may be minimal or elaborate, depending on the artistic ability of the individual. Similarly, for the 'Karva Chauth' (fast for the well-being of husbands) drawing, the feet of the goddess, the moon peeping through a large banyan tree and seven married women shown standing in a row, are essential components. The facial features of the women may be clear but more emphasis is given to elaborating their married status. All the women are bedecked as newly married brides. The wall drawing also shows a *Karva* (earthen pot).

It is also customary to make a wall drawing on the occasion of Diwali. This drawing has

the sun, moon, Shiva, Ganga, Parvati, Ganesha, Lakshmi, Hati Kamal, Shravan Kumar, Chhabaria, Tota and other images. In the Diwali drawings, the main goddess is shown with five heads in the centre. On the occasion of Nag Panchami, the cobra is drawn on the main entrance. Snakes are generally depicted in black on a white background. On Raksha Bandhan (the festival cementing the brother-sister bond), walls on both sides of the door are smeared with red ochre, and the swastika symbol is painted on too.

It is customary to indulge in wall drawings during the nine-day Navratri festival around March-April and September-October. The main drawing for this festival in the Brij area consists of a cave with two staircases on both the sides. Two arms and feet and two faces, one each of Shiva and Parvati, give this cave anthropomorphic features. The other figures here include Nandi, the bull, as well as small temples.

The most illustrious wall drawings are of *kohbar*, a tradition practised in eastern Uttar Pradesh and north Bihar. There are three types of *kohbar*. The *kohbar* of north Bihar is popular as the Madhubani style of painting, described in detail in the section on Madhubani paintings. The *kohbar* of eastern Uttar Pradesh has wall drawings done with rice powder and turmeric, while the border drawings have creeper motifs. The other figures are *chirai mangar* (bird on a branch), *banjara* (human form), *chaukput* (geometric pattern), *navagraha*

(nine planets), *sat sinhani* (seven tigresses), *panch ya saat hathi* (five or seven elephants), *shankh* (conch), *charka* (wheel), *gada* (mace), *padam* (lotus), *devi devata* (gods and goddesses), *juti juta* (married couple), and so on.[vii] These local styles of paintings abound with a variety of forms and are added to the main drawing by the individual artist.

There is an annual calendar of the different types of paintings to be drawn on each occasion. This calendar may vary from region to region. The folk paintings from Brij in Uttar Pradesh include *thape*, *alpana*, *satiya*, and *sanjhi*. There is another style of folk painting in Brij, where Krishna and other characters from Hindu mythology are embellished with gold leaves and semi-precious stones, with a light relief finish. This localized traditional style has become popular in recent years among followers of Krishna around the globe. The Krishna depicted in these paintings is different from the Krishna in Tanjore paintings.

Ritual paintings are a group activity, repetitive in nature, with a predetermined format of space and design and may be practised within the household or outside, as a collective or as an individual activity. These paintings are linked to certain ceremonial rites. Secular paintings are also guided by certain themes, which may in principle be influenced by religious mythology and lore or by individual creations.

The designs linked to the customs, social and ritual practices were divided into two

Facing page:
Krishna stealing butter, glass painting, Thanjavur, Tamil Nadu.

types. Some of the practices emerged as popular ones while others became the lesser practices. The popular practices adapted to emerging trends, and simultaneously continued as traditional rituals. The continuous exposure to the market-oriented client brought about subtle changes in the painted patterns but the basic characteristics of a particular style remained uninfluenced. For example, if the traditional characteristic of the Warli painting is the arrangement and placement of a number of triangles along with lines, dots and circles, it continues to be so because this is the basic character of a particular style. But a number of imaginative or realistic worldviews such as an airplane in the sky or a train are depicted in this style in addition to the traditional themes, signifying the development of folk and tribal paintings for the local and global market. One of the realistic representations is the scene in a rollercoaster by Ganga Devi, painted during her visit to the USA. This painting is in the collection of the National Handicrafts and Handlooms Museum, New Delhi.

Traditionally, the practitioners of folk and tribal paintings have been divided into specific groups. Among the folk and tribal communities of the country, there are two distinct groups of painters. Traditional painters belonging to particular caste groups are known by various names in different regions. They painted the scroll paintings that were used to narrate *Puranic* myths to the villagers. Apart from learning the myths through the painted narrative, the villagers found these visits a major source of entertainment because the ballad singers would move from one village to another carrying these painted scrolls, entertaining and educating the villagers as they moved on. A select group of such painters also painted on ivory, wood and glass.

Tribal paintings are the artistic expressions of tribal communities. Tribes who depict art through pigments are limited in number. They use surfaces like walls, floors and paper to paint on, but some tribal groups, such as the Rathwas of Gujarat, Warlis of Maharashtra, Gonds of central India, and the Gadabas and Saoras of Orissa decorate the walls of their houses. The style of expression may vary from tribe to tribe. For example, among the Warli, the tribe from Maharashtra, there is an emphasis on drawing figures using triangles in different directions. Gond painters create figures by using dots. The Grasia tribals of Rajasthan, who follow Hindu practices, draw the motifs of birds and animals in a style similar to folk motifs.

Folk paintings are generally the group of paintings done by a particular defined caste community, or the womenfolk of the community as householders. These paintings are usually self-sufficient traditions developed independently of other artistic traditions in the region, but there are instances where the folk traditions may be influenced by classical styles of the same region, just as painted murals influence the *kalamkari* and *telengana* paintings. Motifs of folk paintings may also migrate from

Facing page:
Krishna and *gopis*, painted clay relief, Sona Bai Rajwar, Sarguja district, Madhya Pradesh.

one culture to another with the migration of people. One style of folk painting may also have different depictions. The Kayastha, Brahmin and Harijan styles of Madhubani folk painting were traditionally different in their depiction. Now there are merging influences in these styles.

The second group of painters consisted of the women in each community, tribe, caste group and region. These women used pigments in stylized designs to depict a ceremony or simply the well-being of the householder.

Folk paintings are the pictures made in Indian villages, both by women or men, for the decoration of their houses, propitiation of deities or magicoreligious practices. The Kumaoni paintings of Uttaranchal that are made during Janamashtami or Krishna's birthday and portray anecdotes from his life, are one such example. Made with traditional colours on paper known as 'patta' with cotton wrapped on the mouth of a stick, these paintings are deliberately soiled during worship with ghee or oily substances, in order to keep the tradition of this art form alive by repeated re-creation.

The professional painters created the other groups of paintings at the village level. These painters formed a section of the skilled caste group known by different names in different regions, such as *chitrakar* and *patua* in Bengal, *nakkash* in Andhra Pradesh and Rajasthan, *chitrakar* in Orissa and *chitrakathi* in Maharashtra. In these caste groups, which were a part of the Hindu caste system, painting as a family skill

was transmitted in a single line within the family from father to son.

SURFACES

A surface may be two- or three-dimensional and the layout may be vertical or horizontal. The two surfaces, that have been very illustriously used, are the floor and wall. As civilizations progressed, the span of surfaces for painting also increased. Surfaces of clay, terracotta, stone, wood, palm-leaf, fabric, paper, glass and leather emerged as the new materials on which to paint. From primitive times until the present day, painters have used different media as the canvas for their artistic expression. It is important to mention here that the kinds

Facing page: Folk painting, Rajasthan.

Above: Folk painting, Rajasthan.

of tools and pigments vary according to the nature of the surface. Each of the surfaces is required to be prepared or smoothened before painting and the processes for surface preparation also vary from surface to surface.

TOOLS

Painting may be done by three main devices: hands, pieces of fabric, or a *kalam*. The hands include the fingers, palm, and fist. The portion of the hand to be used for executing the painting is dipped in colour and then is applied on the surface. There is a prevalent tradition that the hand is dipped into a colour of turmeric or red ochre and marked on fabric. These impressions, known as *thapa*, are part of an auspicious ceremony during weddings. The hand is used to apply both dry and wet colours. In drawings where powder (dry colour) is used, the colour is picked up between the index finger and thumb and slowly dropped on the surface to form the design.

Fabric or a piece of rag is generally used for wet colours. The technique of applying colour with fabric is called *potana* and is commonly used for fabric painting. The piece of rag may be wrapped on the finger or held in the hand. Similarly, the potter women in Kutch, Gujarat, dip the rag in black colour and smear it on the pot to be painted, while moving the pot. This gives a continuous circular pattern without breaking the rhythm.

Kalam is the Sanskrit word for pen, which is known as a *qalam* in Persian. The basic purpose of a pen is to write and not paint, which is why painting by pen in many folk communities is known as *lekhan*. The *kalam* may be made of metal, reeds, twigs, etc. and is usually created by the artists themselves. The material used to make it depends on the requirements of the job. The *kalam* used in Andhra Pradesh and the Gujarat region for fabric painting is a thick bamboo stick about eighteen centimetres long and six centimetres wide. At a distance of about three centimetres from the tip at one end, a thick coil of goat's hair is coiled and tightly tied. The end of the bamboo stick is the tip of the pen and the thick coil contains the dye. Dye is slowly transferred to the fabric through the tip of the pen.

Another type of *kalam* used for wax painting is an iron loop fixed into a bamboo stick. This is also covered with felt. The *kalam* is dipped in the molten wax and the felt pad absorbs the liquid wax. The gentle pressure on the pad releases the wax down the iron point of the *kalam*, on the required area of the fabric. Another type of pen is the iron pen used for application of pigments made by burning in various oils. The artist picks up the lump of prepared colour known as *roghan*, places it on his palm, then picks up the desired amount with the stylus or iron pen about fifteen to twenty-five centimetres long, and places it on the portion of the fabric to be painted in a chalked pattern. Since the colour is very thick, the stylus helps to form a thread, which is

Palm leaf painting, Orissa.

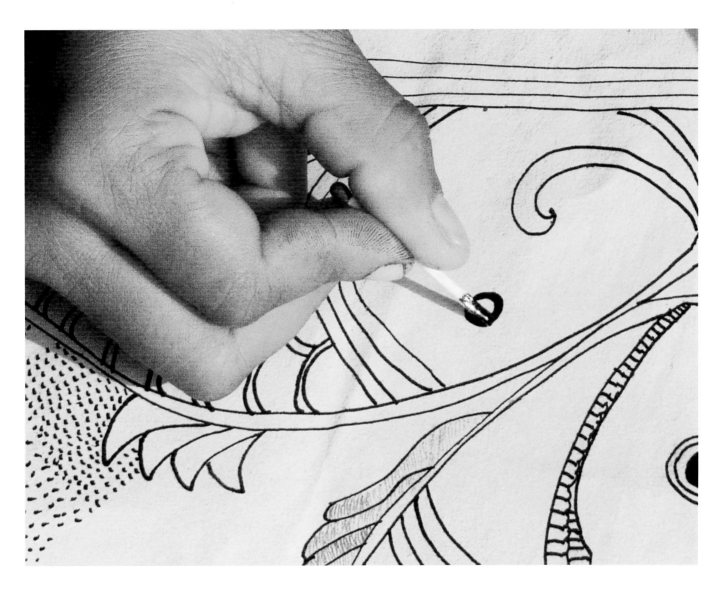

pasted on the fabric when cool. Another series of application of pigments on fabrics is done with a variety of brushes made of animal hair.

Phad painters of Rajasthan, *pat* painters of Andhra Pradesh and *chitrakars* of Orissa use a vast range of brushes. Hair is collected from the ears of a calf for a broad brush, while a medium brush is prepared from hair derived from the underbelly of a goat. A fine brush is made of hair from the tail of a buffalo, while for even finer lines, brushes are made from rat and squirrel hair. In Orissa, brushes for mural painting are usually

Painter applying colour with a *kalam*, Kalamkari, Andhra Pradesh.

made from the root of the screw pine tree. The hair collected from different animals is tied to a strong twig and used according to the strokes required. However, this variety of natural brushes is now slowly disappearing, as many tribal artists prefer using brushes available in the market, made from synthetic fibres.

Women and tribal painters generally use twigs as tools for painting, which can be conveniently discarded once they are used.

PIGMENTS

A vast range of pigments from ordinary lime, red and yellow ochre, lamp soot or lamp black to rice paste, vegetable extractions, minerals and semi-precious stones were traditionally used in folk and tribal painting. The process of fabric painting is technically distinctly different from paintings done on mud floors or walls, wood, stone or ivory. Traditional pigments fall into different groups: earth, mineral, vegetable, animal shells or even bird droppings.

MINERAL PIGMENTS

The important mineral pigments used in India, identified by an analysis of paintings on walls, cloth and paper are described as follows:

WHITE

Calcium carbonate can be found in several forms – chalk is one such form and it has been extensively used to colour paintings. Chalk is found with deposits of limestone and has been used as a pigment by man from a very early time. It is also obtained by grinding shells. In India, conch-shell white was favoured by artists and was believed to have special properties. Some varieties of chalk are very soft and white and are used to derive a pure white colour.

The most important limestone deposits are in Orissa, Bihar, Madhya Pradesh, Rajasthan, Karnataka and Gujarat.

Kaolin, also known as China clay, has been used mainly for preparation of porcelain and for the preparation of pigment in India, where rich deposits of kaolin are available.

Conch-shell white, the distinct bald white, is the colour used by painters in Orissa and Bengal. 'Ka rag' is a high-grade chalk white used in thangka paintings of the Tibetan tradition. The best 'Ka rag' comes from Rinpung, a place located between Lhasa and Shigaste in Tibet.[viii]

Gypsum, with its chemical composition of calcium sulphate, has also been used as a white pigment. The well-known plaster-of-Paris is made by heating gypsum.

White lead is an important pigment used since early times. Chemically, it is the basic carbonate of lead and occurs in nature as *safibda* or *sisa*. However, white lead is usually prepared artificially and then used in paintings. This pigment is used sparingly since it has one fundamental defect, in that it blackens in the course of time.

Zinc white (*safeda*) is another important pigment used for painting. Chemically, it is composed of zinc oxide. According to research scholars, zinc was first described as an element in 1746 in Europe. However, according to archaeological evidence, zinc was known in India, even in very early times and it is quite likely that it was known in India, even before it was introduced in Europe. Zinc white, unlike white lead, does not turn black and so is more extensively used.

Talc, found as a soft stone (or soapstone), is often used as a filler in paints as well as paper. One of its varieties, called *mekol* in the local language, was detected in the wall paintings of Chamba in Himachal Pradesh. There are several varieties of talc, soapstone and steatite available in India from which paints that have good weathering properties can be developed. Bird droppings were also reported to have been used to make white pigment in paintings on the surfaces of rock shelters.[ix]

BLACK

Charcoal black is derived from finely ground charcoal, which is commonly used as a black pigment in India. The charcoal is usually prepared by burning the twigs and wood of the tamarind tree in a closed pot, and the residue is then powdered to make a rich black pigment.

Other substances, which after charring are used for preparing black pigment, are the

Pata painting on paper, Kalighat, West Bengal.

Facing page:
Top: Brushes and colours used by *pata* painter, Orissa.

Bottom: Bhuri Bai, the Gond painter, seen painting a motor car.

73

shells of almonds and coconuts. The charcoal so produced is soft and is used because it gives a homogenous and fine black pigment.

Lamp black (*kajal*) is by far the most important black used in India. It is prepared by burning oil in a lamp and depositing the soot in an earthen bowl.

Ivory black is prepared by charring ivory cuttings in a closed earthen pot and then grinding, washing and drying the black residue. The black so prepared is very intense in colour and texture.

Bone black is obtained by charring animal bones in closed earthen pots. It is not as deeply black as ivory black, but is used as a substitute.

Powdered graphite, a mineral found in different parts of India, has been used as a writing material. It gives a dull grey pigment. However, it has mostly been used for drawing rather than for painting.

Graphite deposits are known to occur in Kerala, Orissa, Bihar, Rajasthan and Sikkim, but it is yet to be seen whether any of these varieties can be useful as a pigment for painting.

Black chalk is the name given to the black clay used for painting pots and terracotta. The clay deposits are collected and soaked in water. Terre-noir is the same as black clay, and is a mixture of carbonate of calcium, iron and manganese with clay.

All these varieties of black, derived from minerals, along with metals like gold (*swarna*), silver (*rajat*), and tin (*ranga*), are also used in Indian paintings.

RED

Cinnabar, also known as native vermilion is a bright red pigment made out of the mineral cinnabar, which chemically is a mercury sulphide compound. Cinnabar, the main ore of mercury, is crushed and ground to make powder, which serves directly as a pigment. It is found in central India.

Artificial cinnabar or vermilion is produced by recombining the elements, mercury and sulphur. This technique was known from very early times. In properties, chemical as well as physical, natural and artificial pigments have the same characteristics.

Red ochre (*geru*) is a pigment abundantly used in Indian painting, and its deposits are found in almost all parts of India. The colour of red ochre is not as bright as that of cinnabar, but it is found in several shades of red. Its use in India dates from very early times and this can be gauged from the fact that red ochre is also known as Indian red. The anhydrous oxide is red, while the hydrated varieties range from red to dull yellow. This is a very stable compound and is not affected by light and alkalis. Red oxide is also produced artificially and there are hardly any differences, chemical or physical, between the two varieties, except that the artificial variety is very finely divided and is homogeneous.

Fine red ochre is obtained by washing and levigation of the crude variety. Levigation is the process in which colour is freed from

impurities by repeatedly adding water to the colour and draining out all the impure elements.[x] Red lead (*sindur*) is not found in mineral form but is made by heating litharge, which is yellow monoxide of lead, or white lead, and is the compound called lead carbonate. Nowadays, it is commercially obtained directly by the oxidation of lead.

The pigment thus obtained is bright red and has been used in Indian paintings in abundance. However, on prolonged exposure to light and air, it turns brown or black. This phenomenon has been observed in most paintings that have been examined in Rajasthan. The same phenomenon was also noticed in the paintings of Kerala. Paintings in other areas in which the bright red pigment is used are yet to be examined.

Lead-ores occur chiefly in the Himalayas, Rajasthan, Bihar and peninsular India. Realgar (*manasila*), a mineral, is found with orpiment, which is also a mineral but yellow in colour. Both are sulphides of arsenic. For some reason, realgar has not been used much in paintings.

Other red pigments:
Besides these mineral pigments, some dyes have also been used for paintings. However, they are not of mineral origin and are derived from plants or insects.

Five-headed Ganesha, wall mural, Kerala.

Facing page:
Painted terracotta pitcher, Gujarat.

Sulphides of arsenic, orpiment, and realgar, form small deposits in Chitral and in Kumaon, Himachal Pradesh. Arseno-pyrites occur near Darjeeling, in the Bhutan Valley and also in Kashmir.

YELLOW

Yellow ochre (*ram raj*) like red ochre, is one of the most important pigments used from the earliest times. In yellow ochre, the colour is on account of the presence of various hydrates of iron oxide, particularly the mineral goethite. The pigment is prepared from natural earth by selection, grinding, washing, levigation and drying. Since it is a natural product, it is found in a number of shades.

Artificial ochre is prepared by precipitating a mixture of soluble iron salt or ferrous sulphate and alum or aluminium sulphate with an alkali-like lime or potash. The proportion of alum used can control the depth of the yellow colour. The final product is a mixture of ferric and aluminium hydroxides and gypsum. On heating this yellow pigment, various shades of orange, red, brown and violet are obtained.

Other yellow colouring materials:
Orpiment (*harita*) gives a brilliant, rich lemon-yellow colour and is a fairly good covering powder. Chemically, it is the yellow sulphide of arsenic as a natural stone. The mineral is found in many countries, including India.

Besides being used as a pigment, it was also used to tint paper, a process that imparts an insecticidal property to the paper. Because of its poisonous character, orpiment is used in a very limited way. The stone is ground into a fine powder and made into a thick paste by adding a little water. Glue is added to the paste, which is then made into small tablets and dried. When the painting is to begin, the tablet is dissolved in water or a wet brush for the thick work is rubbed on the tablet when the colour is used. Some organic materials used to get Indian yellow (*peori* or *gogoli*) are gamboges (gum resin), saffron, turmeric and safflower.

GREEN

Green pigment is obtained from terre-verte (green earth or *harabhata*), malachite (danafarang) and verdigris.

Among the green pigments, terre-verte has been the most widely used since very early times. It is found all over India but only certain varieties are suitable for use as a pigment. In its composition, there are mainly two related minerals, namely glauconite and celadonite, which are hydrous iron, magnesium and aluminium potassium silicate. The colour of green earth, depending on its source, varies from place to place, the shades ranging from yellow green to greenish grey. On heating, the green is transformed to reddish brown. Nowadays, artificial mixtures of pigments giving green earth shades are available but

Tattoo painting, Chhattisgarh.

Verdigris was a common pigment used in Mughal and later miniature paintings. It was also used on textiles. It is prepared by the action of vinegar on copper foils. In composition, it is the normal acetate, or one of the basic acetates, of copper. The pigment obtained is a very bright and deep green. However, it suffers from a great defect, namely, it chars the paper or the textile on which it is used. In that respect, it is necessary that research is conducted to find out how to make this pigment more durable. Although verdigris is commonly believed to be green, it is possible to obtain shades ranging from grey to deep green, by reacting copper strips with vinegar.

BLUE

Blue is obtained from indigo, lapis lazuli, azurite and smalt.

Indigo (*nil* or *neel*) is a vegetable colouring material, which is by far the most important pigment used for painting as well as for dyeing. The plant indigoferra gives the blue dye. In 1880, the process for making synthetic indigo was discovered. These days, synthetic indigo has almost replaced the vegetable variety, but there is great scope for preparation of natural indigo in India. This is another area needing systematic study.

Lapis lazuli is added to pulverize blue colour. Ultramarine blue (*lajwarda*) is obtained from the mineral lapis lazuli, which is a semi-precious stone. It has been used in miniature

their durability is much less. Emerald (*selu*) green is sourced from copper acetoarsenite, an artificial pigment first synthesized in 1814.[xi]

Malachite is another important green pigment. Chemically, it is basic copper carbonate and is found in association with copper ore. To prepare the pigment, the stone is carefully selected, ground and sieved. This pigment is used for *pichhvai* paintings.

Copper occurs in Singhbhum and Chhota Nagpur in Bihar, Nellore and Krishna districts in Andhra Pradesh, Ajmer, Khetri, Alwar in Rajasthan and in the outer Himalayas, in Sikkim, Kumaon and Nepal.

The copper ores change into malachite, azurite and other substances because of various surface alterations.

paintings, *pichhvai* and *phad* paintings of Rajasthan in India. It is said that lapis lazuli was imported to India from Afghanistan. However, it is possible that lapis lazuli may be available in India also.

Azurite (*syama*) is a blue pigment derived from the mineral azurite, which is a chemical composition of basic copper carbonate. Like malachite, it is associated with copper ore deposits. This pigment is used for *pichhvai* paintings. This mineral must also be found along with the Indian copper ores, but it is to be seen whether it can be collected for preparation of the natural pigment, azurite. Artificial azurite has also been produced and is commonly known as blue verditer. The synthetic variety, however, is not as durable as the natural variety.

Smalt (*selu*, *asmani*), another pigment made by a chemical process, is used for the *pichhvai* paintings of Rajasthan.[xii]

Many contemporary painters, including Jamini Roy, were inspired by folk traditions and incorporated the styles in their own paintings. Even within urban metropolises, cities and large towns, there are pockets of art practices which are termed as folk paintings. The creative output of people even within the cities has till recent times not received the same levels of recognition that have been bestowed upon the painters and paintings associated with the Mughal or provincial courts, or individual artists. We bring our own wisdom to pass judgment upon cultures, which exist among and alongside us, but which are not integrated into what we consider as the mainstream of painted art.

Today, folk and tribal painters have found new platforms for themselves. Without the benefit of formal education in schools and colleges of art, they paint with individual imagination, without deviating from their traditional styles, even though the surface, pigments and sometimes even the tools for execution may have changed. The identity of these paintings now resides in the execution style of each painting. The emerging demand from tourists and the awakened interest among the urban elite have contributed to a growing recognition of these distinct individual styles. This is what keeps these groups of paintings a class apart from individual works of artists coming out of contemporary art schools.

Mahisasurmardini, or Goddess Durga, painted in the Madhubani style, Madhubani, Bihar.

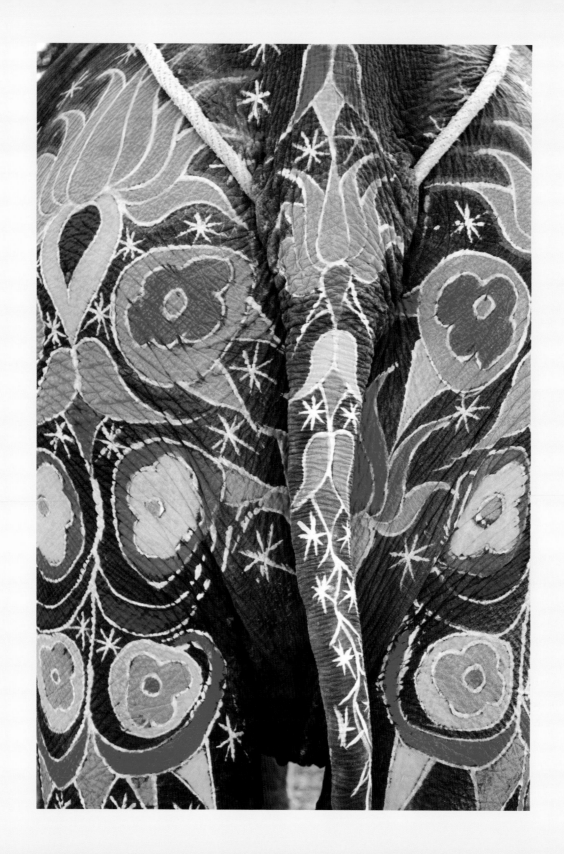

IDENTITIES

We have talked earlier about the concepts related to sacred and secular themes. Identities are the conventional frames of folk and tribal creativity, which may be sacred or secular in theme. Sacred themes have been grouped into iconic and demi-iconic styles, while secular paintings are placed in non-iconic styles. In this chapter, we will discuss some identities in iconic, demi-iconic or non-iconic styles, which are now lesser or forgotten practices in the mainstream.

ICONIC STYLES

Iconic styles of painting prospered around the centres of pilgrimage of a particular religion or religious cult. Jaya Appasamy has recognized this style.[i] The theme of the painting may be the deity itself, or other secular themes reflecting the local culture. The three iconic centres recognized by Appasamy are Nathdwara in Rajasthan, which has the painted *pichhvai* tradition, the Jagannath temple in Puri, Orissa, where the paintings revolve around the Jagannath, also known as Nila Mahadev, and the Thanjavur paintings emerging from the Tirupati temple, where devotees from Andhra Pradesh, Tamil Nadu and Karnataka converge. There is also a fourth centre of iconic painting, which is the Kali temple in Calcutta, West Bengal. Here, apart from the iconic images of Kali, the goddess, the painters also started painting and selling other themes. Under iconic paintings, therefore, we are discussing the *pichhvai* paintings of Rajasthan, Puri paintings of Orissa, Thanjavur paintings of Tamil Nadu, and the Kalighat paintings of Calcutta.

Facing page: Secular painting on the trunk, tail and body of an elephant – an interesting surface.

○ PICHHVAI PAINTING

Pichhvai paintings, as the name indicates, are the painted backdrops, which are used as the temple cloth behind the main icon of Krishna, the incarnation of Vishnu. These painted, embroidered or printed cloths serve the same function as the frescoes on temple walls. Nathdwara, in the Udaipur district of Rajasthan, is an important centre of Vaishnava worship, where the painted *pichhvai*s are made by the artists. The technique used for *pichhvai* painting is similar to the technique used by the scroll painters or the *phad* painters of Rajasthan. The themes of the paintings in the Nathdwara *pichhvai* tradition remain centred around Krishna, who is depicted in the middle of the painting as a black figure with massive compactness. The face prominently features silver lotus eyes, which catch the attention of the worshipper. He is shown wearing a diamond nose-pin, a vermilion mark on the forehead, with one arm raised towards the sky, and the other holding his flute. He wears a knee-length skirt or *dhoti*, his head is adorned with a crown, and his arms, fingers, feet and toes are heavily bedecked with jewellery. The ornaments worn around the neck, including a garland, reach to his feet. Krishna in these paintings is depicted as a stronge, powerful standing image. There is a delicate emphasis on the detailing of decorations on the costumes worn by other characters depicted in the painting.[ii] Apart from Krishna as the central figure, there are several other subjects, which form the thought and content of the paintings. The subject matter varies according to the seasons and the ceremonies for which the paintings are intended to be used. The grandeur of the festivities is well reflected in these spectacular cloth hangings. Some typical themes are *sarat purnima* (full moon night), *varsha* (rainy season), Maharasa Lila (the cosmic dance, where Krishna is shown dancing individually with several women, including his consort Radha) and Mount Govardhan (here Krishna is shown lifting Mount Govardhan[iii] for the protection of the local population from the devastations caused by heavy rains).

The *varsha pichhvai*, for instance, depicts the *kadamba* tree (*Anthocephalus cadamba*), with a vine creeper entwined around its stem. The creeper is the symbolism of serpent power, and is shown on the right and left axes of the spine, while the tree is the *merudanda* or the ethereal nerves. The *varsha pichhvai* is the representation of yogic powers and the depiction of Krishna as the tree-dweller. The painting shows eight companions of Krishna offering items of daily use to the tree. The *kadamba* tree is a constant feature in the life of Krishna. In his childhood escapades, he is said to have hidden in the branches of a *kadamba* tree to avoid a scolding; it is in the branches of this tree that a playful Krishna hides the clothes of the *gopis* bathing in the river Yamuna. Krishna has also been named as *vrikshachari* or the tree-dweller. Men, women, cows, and milkmaids, all form a part of the painting, with Krishna as the central figure. In the Nathdwara

pichhvais, the deity is decorated with the colours, flowers and ornaments reflective of the seasons, which continue to change in harmony with the cyclic movement of nature. In some _pichhvais_, a hundred liquid-eyed cows are shown surrounding their lord, replacing the _gopis_, the milkmaids of Vrindaban.[iv]

Pichhvai paintings are done on fabric, which is prepared by pasting it with wheat flour and glue mixed with copper sulphate. The cloth is dried and burnished with an agate stone. Pasting requires skill as it has to be done in one go to ensure that there are no air bubbles. Squirrel hairs are used to make brushes of various sizes by the artists themselves. The brush is replaced immediately if the painter is not satisfied with the quality. Since the themes of _pichhvai_ paintings are repetitive, the drawings are made from

Painted backdrop showing Krishna, serpents and Lord Brahma.

tracings of existing paintings. The drawings are sized with *kharia* or chalk white. This use of chalk white was also prevalent in the wall frescoes, where kaolin or gypsum (calcium carbonate) was used as the wall plaster for painting. *Babul ki gond* or gum acacia is used with the pigment. The pigments include earth pigments, mineral colours and mineral metals.

○ **PURI PAINTINGS**

The next sequence of *pata* paintings are from Orissa. They have been continuously in existence for almost 300 years,[v] but there are very few deviations in themes in these paintings from Puri.

The themes of *pata* scrolls generally centre around the Krishna legend, as there is a myth that Krishna was killed by a Savara tribal and his heart, which was not consumed by the fire, was thrown into the sea – it was recovered on the seashore at Orissa, where it was turned into a blue stone known as Nila Madhva.[vi] The legend is linked to the tribal worship of Krishna and the images are also in his anthropomorphic form. However, the depictions on scrolls have very stylized characterizations as well as folk visualization. The depiction in the paintings include festivals, such as Sri Krishna Janam (the birth of Krishna), Sri Krishna Leela (narrative of Krishna's life), Sri Krishna Vivah (the marriage of Krishna) and the Dola Yatra and Rath Yatra (the spring and chariot festivals of Orissa).

The Orissa *chitrakar* or painter has a unique technique of preparing the *pata* for painting. In the late nineteenth century, the canvas was prepared by smearing it with a paste of black earth and cow dung. After drying, a white coating was applied to cover the pores of cloth. Nowadays, the cotton cloth is first washed thoroughly to remove the starch and a coating of gum made from the powder of tamarind seeds is applied on the fabric. A second layer of cloth is pasted and another layer of gum applied. The fabric is then allowed to dry in the sunlight. When the fabric is totally dried, soft white stone powder is mixed with tamarind gum in the proportion of 1:4 and this glutinous paste is rubbed on the dried cloth with a cotton puff. Chalk powder is applied on the other side. This base is known as '*pata astra*'. It is cut into the required rectangular or square sizes and it is ensured that there is no wastage. The individual pieces are burnished with a small coarse stone or vitrified brick. A second burnishing is done with a smooth pebble. The burnishing is done on both the sides but the surfaces on which the painting is to be done is further polished with the smooth pebble.

Thus, we see that the preparation of the canvas in the Orissa scroll paintings is most tedious and needs painstaking work. Once the canvas is prepared it is turned on its sides and trimmed. The trimming process is known as *kadamara*. This entire job of polishing and burnishing is generally done by women.

Five primary colours – white, yellow, black, blue, red – and a sixth colour, grey, in different shades are used for the *pata* paintings of Orissa. Different shades are obtained by mixing the primary colours. A description of colours is to be found in several seventeenth-century texts in the Oriyan language.[vii] The colours, which are prepared from vegetable extracts and minerals, are mixed with glue as a binding pigment. The colour white is made from conch shells, black with lamp black, red with cinnabar, lac from dye, and red from ochre. Yellow is made out of orpiment, which is a sulphide of arsenic and is found as a natural stone. The stone is ground into a fine powder and made into a thick paste by adding a little water. The glue is added to this paste and made into small tablets and dried. When the painting is required to be done, the tablet is dissolved in water or a wet brush is rubbed on the tablet for using the colour. The colour blue is prepared from indigo, which is available in tablet form in the market. Adding lapis lazuli, also used for blue, pulverizes the blue colour. These days, several colours are bought from the market.

The *chitrakars* of Orissa have many varieties of brushes for fine as well as thick work. For broad brushes, hair is collected from the ears of a calf. The medium brush is prepared from hair from the underbelly of a goat. Hair from a buffalo's tail is used to make a fine brush, while still finer lines are drawn with brushes made from rat and squirrel hair. The *chitrakars* of Orissa also make mural paintings, for which they use brushes made from the root of the screw pine. Hair collected from different animals is tied together with a strong twig to make the brush. Nowadays, however, the art of making brushes has almost disappeared, and the Oriyan *chitrakars* use brushes available in the market.

Oriyan *chitrakars* still do not use a pencil to make the first sketch but draw the sketches by brush strokes in ochre colour. There is a definite pattern of work when the sequences are painted on the fabric. The first procedure is the demarcation of the border. The second stage is *tipana* or sketching. This is an important task, where the senior, experienced painters draw the sketch from the head, then add a torso and legs. Feet are generally not sketched. Senior artists have a sketch book, which is used as a reference for the figures. Since there is very little deviation from the traditional images, sketches remain confined to limited images.

The next stage is '*hingola banka*', where spaces outside the sketched figure are filled with flat red colour or ochre. This is followed by '*ranga banka*', where the *pata* colours are painted. Here, the application of colour is done to prescribed norms for a particular deity, such as black for the face of Krishna. The garments are coloured next, followed by ornaments. The procedure of colouring ornaments is known as '*gahnalekha*'. This is followed by colouring the areas requiring black known as '*mota kala*'. Next is the process of '*sarakala*', which means the etching of thin black lines that outlines the picture.

After the painting is complete, white touches are given and borders are painted. The work of border painting is done by those painters who are not good at figure work and generally, there are few painters who are skilled in border painting. The painting is reviewed before lacquering and if there are any defects, these are touched upon. The lacquering process is known as '*joshala*'. The painting is held over a smouldering fire of charcoal in an earthen pot. Lac and resin powder mixed in a proportion of 1:3 is sprinkled over the painted surface, and as the powder melts, it is rubbed over the entire surface of the painting with a cotton swab. The other process of lacquering involves heating a lac stick till it starts to melt and rubbing it on the painting. These days, lacquer paint available in the market is also used for lacquer finishing.

○ **THANJAVUR PAINTINGS**

The traditional Thanjavur paintings are in iconic style, which is more direct and entirely religious. Although the contemporary Thanjavur style seems to have originated from Tirupati, where devotees from Andhra Pradesh, Karnataka and Tamil Nadu offer their prayers, there are similiarities in content, which indicate that it may also have originated from the Vijayanagar paintings.[viii]

The Thanjavur painters traditionally belong to the Telugu-speaking Raju community, who are Kshatriyas in the caste hierarchy. The Kondapalli toy-makers of Andhra Pradesh and the painters of the wooden tablets or cloth paintings are said to have migrated to this region from Rajasthan in the eighteenth century. There is continuity in these painted forms from Karnataka to Andhra Pradesh. The surface span of such paintings ranges from temple walls in large towns, walls of houses, wooden panels and sometimes, the fabric panel. A separate series of glass paintings from Tanjore has an independent identity.[ix] While conducting

Orissa painting under preparation, showing Rama, the Hindu god.

Wall mural showing Shiva and Parvati, Kerala.

fieldwork in the southern states, I learnt that after Independence, this painter community largely took to painting the larger-than-life painted mounts of political leaders and actors in order to earn a livelihood, which they could no longer get from their traditional work.

The composition of Thanjavur paintings is static and the centrally placed deity commands the space, with a minimum of narrative or illustrative detail. The central deity is housed within an enclosure of a temple pavilion. There are no background paintings behind the icons. The outer panels of the temple pavilion have only limited borders as heavy encrusted decorations make the space compressed. The forms of deities are robust and show rotundity and massiveness.

The colours used in Thanjavur paintings range from strong blue, deep green and red backgrounds, with the main icon in white, yellow, green or blue. The two combinations of red and blue or red and green, overpower the colour composition. The colours are pure and flat without any mixed shades. The differentiation from one colour to another is marked by surface decorations. The heavy

gem-set style plays a major role in the paintings of later years to make them appear as gigantic ornaments.

The main characteristics of Thanjavur paintings are the gilding and the gem-set technique. Gold leaf and precious and semi-precious stones are luxuriously fixed to depict the jewels and dresses worn by the icons. The child Krishna is an important icon in these paintings, and the crystallized form of baby Krishna is seen in the paintings on glass in the Thanjavur tradition. The early Thanjavur paintings did not use gold as extravagantly as the later pictures. The reason perhaps could have been that these paintings were used in the worship area for embellishment and may have sometimes substituted the bronze images generally used for worship. The use of gold embellishment in paintings was also found in Mughal, Rajasthani, Brij (the area around Delhi), Avadh and Deccani paintings. The application of thick colours on glass, papier mâché and wood in geometric patterns, both iconic and non-iconic, was found prominently in the folk style paintings of these areas till the early twentieth century.

Painting showing Christian art.

A single sheet of jack tree wood is the preferred surface for painting in Tamil Nadu, and the paintings thus produced are called *palagai padam*, that is, pictures on wood. A cardboard sheet is pasted on a wooden base with gum made of tamarind seeds. One or two layers of cardboard are pasted on wood. A piece of cloth is then smeared with *sudha* or the white made of lime. Several layers of white are applied on cloth, and then the surface is smoothened by rubbing it with a shell or polished stone. This is the prepared surface ready for drawing with a brush. All the details, including the places where the gems are to be set, are indicated in this preliminary drawing.

A type of glue called *sukkan* is applied in the areas where gold or gems are to be pasted. *Sukkan* consists of finely ground limestone that is mixed with glue to make it a sticky paste. The stones or gems consist of cut-glass gold leaves, which are embedded in the prepared surface, and more *sukkan* is applied on the peripheries. The intervening spaces are also decorated with an application of *sukkan* to give it a plastic relief quality. Gold paper is cut in fine strips and pasted on this surface raised with *sukkan*. However, for pasting, a thick glue of tamarind seed is used. After the gold and the gem-setting work is done, the colours are applied. The areas with gold may be flat or have an embossed effect, but the application of colours is flat all over. A brush made of squirrel hair is used to apply the glue chalk powder.

The general impression that the Thanjavur style of painting is practised at Thanjavur is not correct. Actually, this style of painting is essentially of Tamil origin and is practised in districts like Kumbhakonam, Trichy, Pudukokkay, and Chikknaikanpettai of Tamil Nadu. The pictures of daily worship, particularly featuring Krishna, such as the child Krishna sucking his toe or with a pot of butter, were produced in very large numbers on wood. Glass as a surface for painting was introduced as part of the British influence. During British rule, portrait paintings of royal families were also done in the Thanjavur style.

There has been a recent revival of Thanjavur paintings done in a smaller or reduced size. These smaller frames are cost-effective for a large number of devotees, and are popular with non-resident Indians settled abroad, particularly those from southern India.

The Thanjavur style of Tamil Nadu has strongly influenced Mysore paintings too. Mysore paintings of Karnataka are an extension of the Thanjavur iconic style and also feature Hindu deities, with heavy and rounded figures, which are filled with flat colours. These paintings are primarily made for walls of *puja* rooms. Rich, vivid colouring, often complemented by gold, gemstones and stylized modelling are prominent features. Jewels, drapery, pillars and canopies are worked in slight low relief with special plaster and the impact that the materials have in a darkened room is that of a glowing presence.

Apart from the individual painted panels on wood, there has been a tradition of lateral, folding doors, numbering six on each side. The central panel has a deep relief figure of Vishnu, the presiding deity of Tirumali Tirupati, flanked by smaller figures of Rama and Krishna, the two other incarnations of Lord Vishnu, which are elaborately painted in other styles. Generally, the folded doors show the details of other incarnations and several episodes from the life of Vishnu in his incarnations as Rama and Krishna.

Wall mural showing a ten-armed goddess, Kerala.

○ **KALIGHAT PAINTINGS**

During the late nineteenth and twentieth centuries, the *chitrakars* at the Kalighat temple in Calcutta began executing paintings in

produced around the Kalighat temple in the Kalighat area of Calcutta, they were given this name by the painter Mukul Dey at the beginning of the twentieth century.

Kalighat paintings are essentially colour and brush drawings created with the 'dab' technique. The colours are applied to the surface with a piece of crumpled rag or a coarse brush cut to a flat edge, in such a way that the colour forms asymmetrical dabs[xi]. After the colour thus applied has dried, the accentuated parts of the body are highlighted with a contour line generally in black, but sometimes in silver colour obtained from the colloidal form of tin.

Mahisasurmardini, or Durga killing the buffalo demon, Kali trampling on Shiva, the families of Shiva, Krishna, Balarama, Kartikeya, and Rama in battle with their sons, are among the religious themes of Kalighat paintings. Interestingly, many of these religious paintings show the influence of the Company School (influence of European thought on Indian expressions of folk art). For example, Hindu gods like Kartikeya are shown wearing shoes and a hat. A man buying fish, a barber cleaning a man's ear, and the portrait of a woman are a few of the secular themes[xii] used in Kalighat paintings.

DEMI-ICONIC STYLES

Demi-iconic styles of painting include groups of paintings which have thematic depictions of Hindu gods and goddesses and local deities

Moving vehicles, particularly public transport, such as trucks, rickshaws, and three-wheelers are painted in popular art. This truck shows painted foliage in bright colours.

square or rectangular frames with stylized icons of several Hindu gods. They also painted characters from everyday life, such as aristocratic Bengali families, Englishmen and other themes. These secular themes were painted in swift black lines with a rhythmic flow. The Kalighat style was the first one to be noticed by the Europeans and became popular as bazaar paintings.[x] Since these works were along with some secular themes. They do not prosper around a pilgrimage centre. Demi-iconic paintings may be in the form of scrolls and leaflets on fabric, paper, wood or glass. Most wall and floor drawings form a part of this category. Demi-iconic wall paintings are practised by tribals also.

There are two distinct segments of painters associated with demi-iconic paintings: one is the identified caste groups, while the other segment consists mainly of women, who paint on the walls and floors for religious and festive occasions. The paintings done by both the groups have a religious tenor. The paintings done by select caste groups of painters in Rajasthan, Andhra Pradesh, West Bengal and Maharashtra are generally taken to various villages either by the painters themselves or by the entertainers. The themes of these paintings broadly focus on local myths, legends, folklore and classical Hindu epics such as the *Puranas*. The paintings done by women are confined to spaces of walls and floors within the village. In this section, we will discuss: firstly, the painted traditions of the select caste groups on different materials; secondly, the traditions of painting on the confined spaces of walls and floors; and lastly, we will talk of painting on miscellaneous materials.

○ SCROLLS AND LEAFLETS

Scrolls and leaflets are depictions from *Puranic* mythology or local legends, but these are not usually found around religious centres. The makers of the scrolls or leaflets generally belong to a specific caste group.

□ PAINTED SCROLLS

Pata or scroll painting is done by the traditional caste-based painter communities. Scrolls may be vertical or horizontal and the stories or themes thus painted are depicted like scenes from a film. Vertical scrolls are unrolled downwards, section by section, according to the scene or sequence being described, the narration thus moving vertically downwards. Bengal, Andhra Pradesh, and Gujarat have traditions of vertical scrolls. Horizontal narrations move sideways, from right to left, and are found in Maharashtra. *Phad* paintings in Rajasthan are done on a horizontal scroll of cloth and are used by itinerant priests, who travel from village to village narrating stories of legendary heroes through mime and song. The scrolls are unrolled and held at both the ends by people. The *bhopa* or singer-performer highlights the section which is being narrated, with a lamp. Since the performance is held at night, other sections of the scroll are not visible to the audience.

Pata painting as a folk tradition is perhaps one of the earliest painted art forms, which were prevalent in India before the arrival of the Aryans. In Sanskrit, 'pata' means cloth made of jute. Similarly, in the tribal languages of the Santhalis and Mundas, the word *pata* means jute fabric. *Pata* also conveys the sense

Lamp black and traditional *kalam* made of reeds are the tools used for drawing in Madhubani painting.

of a canvas. These paintings may be on fabric or on paper. Some regional variations of painted scrolls on fabric and paper are described here.

PATA CHITRA: WEST BENGAL

Traditionally, in West Bengal, *pata chitra* was the term used for long scroll paintings. These folk paintings, also known as 'samajik pata', include both religious and secular subjects. The religious themes usually depict stories from the Mahabharata, but sometimes Muslim and Christian themes are also included. Religious *patas* depict important incidents from the religious texts. The characters are visualized either in a forest or in a palace or residential area. Human characters occupy the main space of the canvas. Spontaneous lines drawn by *patuas* have an angularity, and anatomical details are not very defined. The secular *pata chitras* depict political events, natural disasters and also many popular characters. Local events play an important role in secular *pata chitras*. For instance, the tsunami disaster in 2004 has recently emerged as one of the important themes for the *pata* painters. The late Prime Minister, Indira Gandhi, was idolized as the goddess Indira in *pata chitras*. The sequences in the panels depicted episodes from her childhood, marriage and motherhood, right up to her assassination.

The communities who are painting *pata chitras* are known as *patuas* in West Bengal. They are also known locally as *patidat, patekar, pateri,* or *paitkar*. Apart from painting pictures on paper, *patuas* also model clay icons and toys. They wander from village to village, singing songs and showing the accompanying narration on paper or jute scrolls. *Patuas* thus sell the painted toys but use the painted scrolls to narrate stories. Contemporarily, these folk painters of West Bengal have started using the term *chitrakar*, which literally means a painter, as a title.

Traditionally, the colours prepared by them included colours from lamp black and vegetable pigments. Their brushes are simple implements cut from the hair of domestic animals like the cat, goat and squirrel.

Another distinct group of *pata* painters is the 'jadu (magical) patuas'. According to a local myth of Purulia and its adjoining areas, it is believed that *jadu patuas* were born of the union of Gazi Pir (a local Muslim saint) and his Hindu wife. The *jadu patuas* traditionally work in brass and bell metal and are so called because the paintings they create are part of the magicoreligious practices concerning a death in the household in the Santhal community. The Santhal tribe recognizes them as 'Jan guru', that is one of the gurus who have magical powers to protect the tribal clans from evil, disease and death. *Jadu patuas* are also considered to have the capacity to send the wandering souls of the dead to heaven and thus help to free them of all pain. There are two groups of *jadu patuas*, namely, the *duari* and *doori patuas*.

Facing page:
This Mysore painting shows Saraswati flanked by two attendants, seated on a throne inside a palace; the rendering of the painting is similar to the miniature technique. The costume attire and the facial features of the deity and attendants reflect the Mysore style.

95

Duari patuas show *pata chitras* from door to door in nearby villages, from morning to evening and return home at night. *Doori patuas*, as the name reflects, travel long distances. Sometimes they return to their homes after a week or so. They are the painters for tribes such as the Bhumias, Kherias and Bedias of the Santhal Pargana region of Bihar and the Purulia district of West Bengal. The themes painted by *jadu patuas* relate to the emergence of the Santhal tribe, scenes from the life of Krishna, Rama, Chaitanya and Satyanarayana, the Hindu gods. Other themes are connected with mountain worship (*paharpuja*). *Chakshudan* is one theme, which is highly important among the *pats* drawn by *jadu patuas*. When a man, woman or child dies, the *duari patua* appears at the house of the bereaved family with a painting, in which the iris of the eye is missing. He shows this picture to the bereaved relatives of the dead and explains that their dear one is not able to see as his iris is missing. However, simultaneously, he also offers an immediate solution. He agrees to paint the iris of the dead after the relatives make him a suitable presentation in the form of money and other articles. It is believed that with the aid of these presentations, the eyesight of the wandering soul is returned.

Other themes painted by *jadu patuas* include *pishacha*, the evil, which causes death in the Santhal community. It is believed that *pishacha* enters a household either through domestic animals or drinking water and the person who drinks that water meets death. Therefore, the *pishacha pata* often shows pictures of animals, water buckets and people of the Santhal community drinking the water.

TELENGANA PAT

Traditional caste-based groups of painters from the Jingor, Muchi and Mera castes were engaged in decorating temples and painting idols, the chariots of the gods and goddesses. These caste groups are known as *nakkash*[xiii] also. Mythological paintings painted by them were used for storytelling, along with idols made from sawdust and wood by storytellers accompanied by musicians. Painted scrolls were used as visuals to illustrate the story sequences. These storytelling sessions often carried on every night for a full week, after which, the audience would present the storytellers with money, cloth and food. The theme and content of the scroll was given by the particular community for which the session was arranged, based on the prevailing myths and legends. These painted themes include Kunapulla Varu – the narration of the birth of the Padamsale or weaver community of Andhra Pradesh, while Markandeya Puran Addapollu, depicts the origin of the Mangali caste group, a Brahmin caste group, and so on. The scrolls were usually about one metre long, with the story painted in forty to fifty horizontal sections. The background colour of the scrolls was generally red.[xiv]

Facing page:
Kartikeya, Kalighat painting.

Chakshudan pat,
paper, West Bengal.

PHAD PAINTING OF RAJASTHAN

Another group of painted scrolls are found in Rajasthan. These scrolls depict the lives of local heroes like Dev Narayanji and Pabuji Ramdevi, who are revered and worshipped in rural Rajasthan. These paintings are called '*phad*' and have an unwritten history of continuity from the time of the miniature painters of Rajasthan. The recognition of *phad* paintings in the court tradition of the provincial courts of Rajasthan went unnoticed perhaps because the painted *phad* was like a mobile shrine. Thus, the *phad* was not seen by viewers other than those who came to worship. These *phad* paintings were traditional and not painted commercially. The decision

to get the *phad* painted was made by the *bhopa* along with his patron. The price of the *phad* was settled by the patron before painting commenced, and the painters began the process only on an auspicious day with a ritual offering to Saraswati, the goddess of learning. The *phad* painters of Rajasthan are scattered in the Bhilwara region, with concentrated pockets in Shahpura, Jaipur and Chittorgarh. The painters assume the title '*joshi*' as they also sometimes paint and illustrate horoscopes. The intimacy of the *bhopa* and *joshi* is reflected in the painted *phad,* with the *bhopa* providing the subject matter. Just as in Andhra Pradesh, the group of artists painting the *phad* is different from the group that narrates the story. Apart from the paintings on cloth, *phad* painters also painted on the mud walls of local shrines. Mud shrines would have a terracotta plaque of the deity to whom the shrine was devoted. An entire wall would have small sectional sequences of the narration running horizontally on both sides of the terracotta plaque. The *bhopa* would sing a particular epic song and his wife, with the help of a lighted lamp, would highlight the sequence on the *phad* referred to in the song. The legends of Dev Narayanji, Pabuji Ramdevi *pir* and Dharamraj are different from each other, therefore the narration varies accordingly. Colours used are similar to the colours for *pichhvai* paintings.

A recent *phad* painting even depicts film actor Amitabh Bacchhan, a contemporary hero, as the central character.[xv]

CHITRAKATHI PAINTING

The states of Maharashtra and Andhra Pradesh have their own tradition of scroll paintings originating from a group of wandering storytellers known as the '*chitrakathi*'. The *chitrakathis* accompany their recitation of the epics with paintings, puppet shows and mime as they move from village to village. Pinguli, a small village in southwest Maharashtra in the Ratnagiri district, about twelve kilometres from Sawantwadi, is the area where the *chitrakathi* tradition survives even today. The paintings are done by a nomadic tribe called Thakkar, said to have migrated to this part of

Maharashtra in the mid-eighteenth century. They might also have settled in other parts of Maharashtra including Nasik, Igatpuri, Miraj and Kolhapur. They also crossed Syadhari to descend into the Konkan region. The occupation of the Thakkar tribe was to travel from village to village and entertain people. While travelling, they also worked as secret information-gatherers for the rulers and had close contacts with the Maratha kings. They also manage to extract political secrets from people while performing the shows.

Chitrakathi paintings are also known as Pratisthan paintings and were presented to the nobles of the Vijayanagar kingdom. Thick and ivory-coloured handmade paper was used for these paintings, which depicted a variety of scenes from the Ramayana, Mahabharata and *Puranas* with local variations. The paintings of the eighteenth and nineteenth centuries project a strong male-dominated culture. The mood of the paintings is fiery, with battle scenes, spirits, and demons generally occupying most of the space on the canvas.

The pictures made on one episode are arranged in sequence and put together in a loose-leaf book form. This book is known as a '*pothi*' and wrapped in a red cloth, which is called a *rumal*.

The *pothi* begins with a picture of Lord Ganesha and one image of this deity is used for several *pothis*. The Thakkar tribe possesses about forty *pothis* and the number of leaves in each *pothi* ranges from forty to sixty. Since the picture on each leaf is pasted back to back, the total number of pictures in a *pothi* ranges from eighty to 120. The square or rectangular frame of leaves are picked up from the *pothi* during the performance and held up for the public to see clearly, just like a contemporary slide presentation.

The earliest group of paintings is about 250 years old, the second group is about 150 years old and the last series is about sixty years old. Since the paintings are on paper, the oldest paintings are in very bad shape. The paintings vary in style and bear a similarity to the paintings of Rajasthan, Andhra Pradesh and Karnataka. *Chitrakathi* painting is a forgotten practice but now efforts are being made to revive it.

KAVAD

A mobile shrine of wood found in Rajasthan, a *kavad* is usually about thirteen to fourteen inches long and six to eight inches wide. These mobile shrines have eight to ten folding doors on each side of the central deity. The narrations on the panels relate to the central deity, which may be Rama or Krishna and the paintings can be seen on both sides of the panels. The central deity is a deep relief carved image. The doors of the *kavad* are left wide open to allow people to pay their homage to the deity. Each of the door panels is divided into three or four horizontal sections and each frame has a painted image depicting a section of the recited narrations. Generally, episodes from the life of Krishna and Rama are displayed on the door panels. The episodes from the *Bhagvata Purana* describing life after death, both in heaven and hell, also form the theme of some paintings. The painting on a *kavad* is lacquered after it is completed.

Kavads were carried on the head by the narrators from village to village. They were painted only on a specific order of the wandering narrators by the *Joshi* painters, who were also engaged in painting scrolls. These groups of paintings were not sold in the market. In current times, small *kavads* with three to four panels are painted for the purpose of decorating the household shrine.

Another tradition of paintings on wood has been seen lately in the Puri paintings, where the deities Jagannath, Subhadra and Balram are shown as deep relief figures in the centre, while single panels of doors show episodes from the life of Krishna.

KALAMKARI

Painted and block-printed scrolls on fabric are the localized tradition in Andhra Pradesh. 'Kalam' is a Persian word (*qalam*) meaning pen, while '*kari*' means art. Therefore, this work is the art of the pen, which is used with finesse by the artists. Kalahasti and Masulipatnam are the two regions where painters, generally from the Baroja caste, practise this art. The technique of *kalamkari* painting is intricate because of

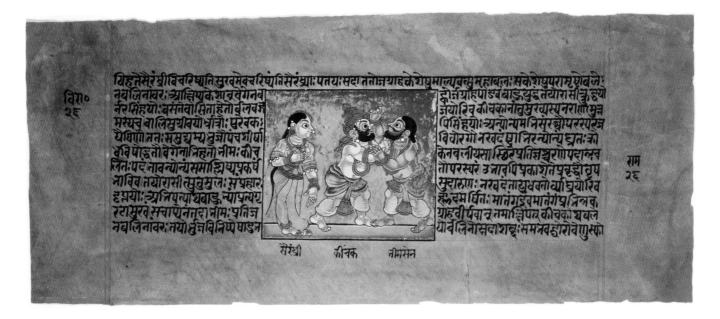

the application of several colours and treatment of the fabric before application of colour.[xvi]

○ **WALL AND FLOOR**

Mildred Archer[xvii] has identified some of the early twentieth-century drawings on walls and floors as Gurgaon paintings since these paintings were collected from Gurgaon in Haryana. Such drawings are part of the magicoreligious practices performed on specific festivals and sacred ritual ceremonies relating to birth and marriage in Haryana, Madhya Pradesh, Uttar Pradesh and Rajasthan. Dr. Vimla Verma[viii] has listed thirty festivals and five sacred ritual ceremonies for Uttar Pradesh and Uttaranchal. The important festivals are Navratri, Nag Panchmi, Raksha Bandhan, Ahoi Ashtami, Karva Chauth, Harchat,

Diwali, Dev Uthan and Ekadashi. Rituals of birth, *chatth* (sixth day after birth), the sacred thread ceremony and marriage are illustrated.

The sun, moon, clouds and serpents are some of the images drawn by the Gond and Baiga tribals of the Mandla region of Madhya Pradesh. Gonds are known as Ravanvanshi or descendants of Ravana, the powerful king of Lanka. But Gonds consider themselves to have originated from Mahadeo.[xix] Tribals also draw images of Hindu gods particularly Hanuman, the monkey god, Ganesha and Mahisasurmardini.[xx] The birth of Krishna is celebrated by the Grasia tribe by drawing Krishna with his *gopis* on the outer walls of their homes. Tribals of the Mandla district in Madhya Pradesh draw stylistic paintings called '*Kanhaiya aathe*' on Janamasthami, the festive

Manuscript painting, paper.

Facing page:
Ramayana panel showing Ravana and Sita in Ashoka Vatika, *chitrakathi* painting, paper, Maharashtra.

celebration of the birth of Krishna. Similar paintings are also drawn by the Ahir and Raut communities of Chhattisgarh.

The Bundelkhand region, comprising Gwalior, Datia, Tikamgarh, Chhattarpur, Jabalpur and the Sagar-Damoh area of Madhya Pradesh, has long-standing traditions of ritual paintings. The folk artists in this area are a caste-based group called *chiteras*, who make drawings of Lakshmi on Diwali in varied styles.

□ SANJHI

It may be debatable whether the use of clay in cow dung instead of colour pigments can be considered a folk painting style or not. But clay and cow dung appliqué designs on the walls are made in Rajasthan, Haryana, Uttar Pradesh and the Bundelkhand and Nimar regions of Madhya Pradesh, once each year. In some parts of Rajasthan, these are drawn with lime paste. These appliqué figures are known as *sanja*, *sanjhi* or *sanji*.[xxi] The vernacular meaning of the term is evening. The significance of these diagrams is that the haunting souls of departed relatives may come and seek shelter in them. The task of making the designs is given to young unmarried girls during the fortnight between the full moon day of Bhadrapad and the no moon night, in the month of Ashvin in the Hindu calendar. This part of the calendar is significantly marked as the *pitrapaksha* or *kanagat*. It is that

time of the year, when all the departed relatives are once again remembered, that is, it is the phase for paying obeisance to the *pitra* or ancestors from the patrimonial side. Feasts are arranged for the priests and no decision regarding a purchase or a marriage is taken during this period. Young unmarried girls keep a fast and perform a final ceremony after the marriage takes place.

Sanjha, who is considered to be the virgin form of Goddess Shakti, is not drawn each day, but only on the occasions mentioned above. The motifs and characters are drawn using white liquid pigments made of rice flour or white lime or else a thick paste of cow dung and clay plaster. A new motif is drawn on each day for fourteen days. The images are decorated with leaves, petals and bangles. Various articles are included in the diagram such as a cone, ladder or palanquin. The last figure drawn is a geometric boundary known as '*kila kot*'. The *sanjhi* drawing is never addressed as a painting. It is referred to as '*sanjhi khelana*'. This signifies that it is a ritual game which is played by making sequential drawings on the walls.[xxii]

□ OSAKOTHI TRADITION

Osakothi is an isolated tradition of wall murals painted by professional painters in Orissa.[xxiii] 'Osa' is a fasting ritual in south Orissa. '*Kothi*' in Oriya is derived from the Sanskrit term '*kosthi*', which means a square or rectangular diagram. Osakothi is therefore the specified

site of 'Osa' rituals. 'Osa' fasting starts from the eighth day of the bright fortnight in the month of Ashvin (September/October) and lasts until Dussehra, the tenth day of the same fortnight. It may extend up to the following full moon night (Ashvin Purnima). The Osakothi mural painting is the specific tradition of the Ganjam district of south Orissa. Another similar tradition known as Dalkhai Kothi is performed in and around Sambalpur in western Orissa.

There are four groups of painters who work on Osakothi murals. These are professional *chitrakars*, painters from the priestly community, the underprivileged Bauri group and contemporary youth.[xxiv] The *chitrakar* community of Orissa paints on cloth, paper and wall surfaces. They also make toys of cow dung and paint narrations on other unique surfaces such as coconuts. From time to time, these painters provide a regular service to the Jagannath temple. We have already discussed important works of this community in the iconic section.

Osakothi shrines are also called '*gramadevati*', the village guardian. The main deity is presented as a *ghata*, the pot, and illustrated in the murals along with several other deities. There is an annual season for Osakothi painting, which lasts for seven to nine days before Dussehra, and generally, the same location is chosen for artists to get together every year. The worshippers of these shrines are from the lower caste, with no Brahmin priest.[xxv] The iconography of the painted themes includes nine forms of the Goddess Shakti, the classical gods, Mangala, a benevolent village deity, *gramadevati*, legendary heroines and heroes, such as Ponchu Pandwa, Navagunjara, Kamadhenu and Hanuman, minor legendary characters and several motifs.[xxvi]

□ SAORA PAINTINGS[xxvii]

Saora is the name of a tribal community inhabiting the hilly areas of the Koraput, Gunpur, Ganjam and Gajapati districts of south Orissa. The paintings of the Saora community are linked to the healing process for disease, safe childbirth and other life events. Sometimes, paintings are also done on festive occasions. The sun, moon, icons of the tutelary spirits, and ghosts, form the content of the paintings. Contemporary motifs such as bicycles, motor cars and aeroplanes are also used. Saora paintings have not been influenced by the Osakothi tradition discussed above, and do not, for instance, include Lakshmi *puja* motifs.

These paintings are done on wall surfaces smeared with red ochre and rice paste. Yellow, ultramarine blue and black are also used at times to enhance the visual effect. No adhesive is added to fix the colours on the wall. Palm twigs are used as brushes for painting, the end of the stick being beaten by the painter to make it fibrous. Icons are drawn by the *kundan*, the village sorcerer. He is also known as Ittalmaran, the professional painter. In the early 1990s, the crafts council of Orissa provided Saora women with paper for painting.

Facing page:
Dev Narayan shrine wall mural showing the narrative of the local hero, Dev Narayan of Bhilwara, Rajasthan.

There were initial problems of imaginative transfer from a vertical to a horizontal surface, but some of the women artists have done it successfully. Despite this, the style of painting has not had the same commercial success as the Warli paintings of Maharashtra.

The other set of wall paintings from south Orissa are Jhoti or Chita. These are the white diagrams on walls and floors drawn with rice paste by women, who make a variety of impressions with their fists, palms and fingers.

☐ OTHER TRIBAL PAINTINGS

The Binjhwars of Raigarh make some of the most beautiful paintings on the walls of their homes during Diwali and at weddings. Unlike the geometrical *chowks* of the Gonds, Kanwars and Baigas, these tribals illustrate simple forms with bold and thick lines. First, they draw a large square joining the corners, thus giving it the semblance of a flower. To portray trees and plants two straight lines are drawn, and in the midst of this huge image, the motifs of the sun, the moon, the swastika, the hooves of cows, and the feet of Lakshmi are painted. The Binjhwars of Bilaspur also decorate the sites of their *karma* and *saila* dances with simple wall paintings. Etmanagar Haldi Bazar of Bilaspur district, Doomaria, Mahendragarh, Sonagara of Sarguja district and Metnagar and Doomarkona of Raigarh district, exemplify some of the most artistic geometrical representations painted on the doors and exterior walls of the houses of this tribe. The boldness of the geometrical figures and the variations of overlapping triangular lines and arches create unusual diamond-shaped motifs. The image of a goddess called Mangala Devi is also painted on the interior walls of these houses.

The women of Chhattisgarh make elaborate votive forms with cow dung on their walls on Hariyali Amavasya, the moonless night, during the month of Sravana (August-September). As a good omen and to safeguard their houses from evil spirits, they draw four furrow-like lines and compose figures on the main entrance of the house. Human figures engaged in activities like hunting, riding and dancing are painted above these lines, while motifs of the sun, the moon, flowers and plants are also portrayed on these lines. These paintings are called '*savanaahi*'.

The hunter tribe, the Kashgharua in Bilaspur, comprises expert painters, who paint colourful images of Mahadeo (Shiva) and Rama on walls, for special occasions.

Votive paintings drawn to celebrate the birth of Krishna, known as *Kanhaiya aathe*, are stylistic paintings, which are painted by mixing *karia mitti* (black soil), *ramraj* (yellow ochre) and *geru* or red ochre, with betel leaf juice by the tribals of the Mandla district of Madhya Pradesh. Paintings in this style are also created by the Ahirs and Rauts of Chhattisgarh. Krishna surrounded with his cows and three to five *gopis* carrying milk pots on their heads, is the theme generally depicted in these paintings.

Facing page:
Karva Chauth painting, on a wall, ritual painting drawn by women at the time of Karva Chauth, a festival in north India, when married women fast for their husbands.

□ DOTS AND LINES

Drawings on the floor are known as 'kolam' in Tamil Nadu, and their place is at the threshold of the house, a zone of passage from the 'known', the interior of the house, to the unknown outside. This zone is protected by the design, which is traced on the floor in an unbroken line forming loops and enclosures, each marked

Hoi painting, a ritual art form drawn by women during a festival in north India when mothers keep a fast for their children.

by a dot in its centre. The dot represents the Mother Goddess and is also a symbol of fertility. Archana Shastri[xxviii] reports that the dominant motif in the villages of Andhra Pradesh is the dot, a series of them arranged meticulously around the inner walls of the house. In Telengana, Andhra Pradesh, and Tamil Nadu, the thresholds are mainly dotted in red and yellow. The vermilion dot is a potent symbol, the archetypal meaning of which is associated with blood, the source of life, and the primordial Mother Goddess. In Andhra Pradesh, the floor tracings are called '*muggu*'. In this state and in Karnataka, the line takes the shape of a serpent, the convolutions of the body of the serpent laid out around its head. The dots here are given the shape of a pentagram.

The dot and the snake are the most potent symbols of fertility and regeneration. The theme of the serpent gives a mythical definition to the wavy lines of the drawing on the floor. They glide with geometrical assurance in and out of the loops of the configurations, which consist of one uninterrupted, continuous linear movement. It conveys the power of the serpent in the goddess, and the dots corroborate her presence.

○ GLASS PAINTINGS

Paintings on glass require a different technique from the paintings on solid opaque surfaces. The pictures on glass are generally in tempera. The brush outlines and the details, which when finished will appear uppermost, are carried out as the first step. This means that in a portrait, the details such as the designs of jewellery and other intricate minutiae are done before applying the colours in the larger opaque areas. In simple terms, we may say that the usual process of painting is reversed. The picture is mounted with the unpainted side of the glass appearing as the outer surface. This technique requires a certain amount of skill and power to retain the visual imagery.

Glass paintings emerged as an outgrowth of the Thanjavur paintings in southern India and Kalighat paintings in West Bengal. In the eighteenth century, glass paintings entered into the royal families but slowly filtered down to popular tradition. The characters in the paintings executed for the royal families were mainly portraits of aristocrats, their mistresses or dancing girls. These distinct styles were perhaps painted for the foreign market. However, it is not certain whether the painters were of Indian or foreign origin.

NON-ICONIC STYLE

The paintings discussed under this section are the practices of both folk and tribal communities, which are not related to any particular mythic cult, but are the practices which are part of decorative traditions. There are several such styles. Generally, these paintings are made with simple earth colours, rice paste and lamp black. Painting and relief work in clay go hand in hand. In many instances, the images created by the clay relief form the centre-stage of the tall canvas of the wall. This is filled with contrasting colours.

○ LIPAI

There are a large number of tribal and folk communities in Raipur, Bilaspur, Durg, Bhilai, Rajnandgaon, Sarguja and the Raigarh districts of Chhattisgarh. The Rajwars, Ahirs, Panka, Satnami and a few other folk communities, and the tribal communities – namely, the Oraon, Nagesia, Kanwar, Badi, Soma, Gond and Pando – decorate their homes with paintings known as '*lipai*'. This is the characteristic painting done by fingers and hand. The area to be painted is plastered with mud and cow dung and then the lines or patterns are etched with fingers.

Rajwar women of Sarguja in Chhattisgarh are proficient in the art of painting and can boast of a rich and exquisite tradition of wall decoration. The mud-plastered wall is dabbed with '*chuhi*', chalk solutions, and quick finger marks are drawn over it. Interweaving vertical, horizontal, diagonal and wavy lines, rendered with a great sense of freedom and rhythm, the women produce a glowing tapestry of white lines on a dull mud surface. This style of wall decoration is similar to the tattoo motifs of the Baigas, who also employ linear forms.

The movement of the fingers in the designs created by the Pando tribe remains restricted

Tulsi is a sacred plant in India and often a permanent platform is built around it. This platform is smeared with mud and usually painted with holy figures. Here, a cow and other motifs are painted in a realistic style, Haryana.

to linear patterns. More colours are added, sometimes to create a multicoloured mosaic design, which appears like a woven fabric. The in-between spaces are at times filled with bud, flower and animal motifs.

The Kharagvanshis and Agarias of the Bilaspur region, however, adorn their houses with elaborate paintings and relief work. They paint a wide network of broad lines in red, yellow and ochre on the entire surface of the wall. First, the whole wall is divided into oblong figures of various sizes and these are filled up

with horizontal, vertical, diagonal and semi-circular lines. Often, the figures are divided into two or three parts, which are merely filled with colours. The doors and windows of their houses are decorated with rows of triangular arches and motifs of birds, animals and fish.

The women of the Ghasiya tribe make simple and bold decorations, mainly with the colour black applied on a yellow ochre plastered wall. People of Pendrapand in the Raigarh area decorate their houses with simple painted borders, embellished with three-petalled white flowers. The *vivah stambha* or wedding pillars of the Korba community are plastered with mud and geometrical motifs, usually triangular, forming a sort of *damru* or drum design.

The Bharia women decorate their houses with centimetre-thick lines embossed on the walls, thus decorating the doors, windows, wall-pegs and small niches. Single and double lines, in circles and squares are embellished with figures of dogs, cats, horses, bulls and rabbits. The four sides of the door are beautifully adorned with parallel lines. These designs are called '*dora*' or '*goh dora*'. Sometimes the '*dora*' patterns follow the shape of the niche and sometimes they spread out like the sun's rays. Other forms include motifs of flowers, flower-pots and birds sitting on trees.

○ **BUDANI PAINTINGS**

The Korko tribal women of Madhya Pradesh decorate their walls with simple and colourful

geometric designs. These paintings are called '*budani*'. The main form of a '*budani chowk*' is made of double lines in an octagonal frame. Closely placed '*budani*' create a beautiful, finely woven network. Sometimes, a large '*budani*' is drawn and divided into several parts. In addition, flowers, flower-pots and creepers are also painted.

○ ROGAN PAINTING OF KUTCH

A non-iconic tradition of painting in Kutch, Gujarat, is known as Rogan, which has striking simplicity in the motifs drawn on one corner, which is then folded and pressed to get printed impressions on the rest of the fabric. The colours are prepared in castor oil and the pen used for drawing is an iron stylus.

○ IVORY PAINTINGS

Painting on ivory was found in many of the provincial schools, such as Bengal, Patna, Rajasthan, Varanasi, Delhi, Deccan, Mysore and Thanjavur. The painters were from the traditional caste groups. Today, ivory is a banned item, and any type of trading or handiwork is not permissible under law. Thus, paintings on ivory have become museum items, and can only be found in the collections of museums such as the National Museum and the National Handicrafts and Handlooms Museum in New Delhi.

The technique of painting on ivory is very different from other materials. The size of the plate depends on the diameter of the elephant tusk, and is small in circumference. The painting itself is limited by the size of the plates. Ivory paintings were not folk paintings in the strict sense, but often used motifs from the folk vocabulary. The ivory surface was prepared for painting by cutting it into a plate of about two- to five-millimetre thickness. The pieces were soaked in water for about eight to ten hours and then these sheets were polished with fine sand or a smooth stone-like agate. The polished pieces were washed once again and stored

Mumtaz Mahal, Mughal queen, ivory painting, Rajasthan.

with decorations in gold, using either gold leaf or gold powder mixed with a gum made from fish. Since the surface to be painted is very small, the painter often used a magnifying glass while painting. Portraits and monuments were an important theme for ivory paintings. Other themes included birds and flowers.

Ivory painting forms a part of the discussion on folk paintings on account of the *ganjifa* or painted playing cards. These playing cards, which are generally on paper or sometimes on wood, are also made of ivory. The small round cards have a thin gold border and a pictorial motif according to the specification of the card. The colours of the cards are dark red, gold and green. For details, refer to the section on the *ganjifa* cards. Resplendent paintings on ivory were very popular for portraiture. With the appearance of photography, however, this style of portraiture slowly disappeared.

A large number of ivory carvers and ivory painters have taken to other professions or have taken to using bone as the base material. Bone carving has been a replacement for the ivory carvers but painting on bone could not be undertaken because of the basic difference between bone and ivory. In modern times, plastic sheets are being used as an alternate material for ivory painting.

○ USTA ART OF BIKANER

The art of engraving and painting done on camel hide is known as the *usta* art of Bikaner.

between sheets of heavy glass so as to avoid any marking. The sketches were either drawn directly on the surface in faint colours or were delicately traced from paper. The colours were generally watercolours applied with a sable hair brush. Since ivory does not crack and can be polished to get a smoothened surface, it was often used for miniature painting.

The other technique of painting on ivory is similar to the folk painting techniques used for wall and fabric paintings. Gum is mixed directly with the colours. There are no brush strokes but the colours are laid on the ivory surface in dots or small strokes. The paintings are embellished

Usta originated in Iran, developed during the Mughal period and came to stay in Bikaner as a part of Indian culture.

○ PAINTING ON MARBLE, PALM-LEAVES AND CLOTH

Painters from Rajasthan also paint on marble. The pigments used are the same as those for miniature paintings. Marble paintings are used for interior and exterior decorations and their themes are inspired by traditional Mughal- and Kangra-style paintings.

Palm-leaf painting of Orissa is made on specially treated palm-leaves. Colours are mixed with country-made glue and inserted into fine engravings by a needle-like instrument on each leaf, producing sharp linear drawings based on themes like Chaitanya, Jagannath, epics and myths.[xxix]

Manipuri painting, based largely on the Radha-Krishna Raas Leelas is a by-product of the Vaishnavite movement and achieved fame in the seventeenth century.

Thangka paintings have flourished in the hill regions of Nepal and Sikkim. Cloth thangkas portray gods, goddesses, demons and dragons, as well as stories from the life of Buddha and the *Jatakas*. Wooden masks and dragon paintings on bamboo are also part of the art of Sikkim. All these have beautifully blended bright colours that are counterbalanced by gold line work and show influences from the styles of Central Asia, China, Japan and the Far East.

The rich diversity of the art forms, whether abstract designs or figurative art, produced by rural and tribal people all over the country, have had a lifespan of thousands of years. Even if contemporary technology and the modern means of communication hinder its practice, it is being revitalized through the recognition of the work of individuals, the repositories of traditional art – among them, Warli artist, Jivya Soma, Ganga Devi, the Madhubani painter and Santokhba, the artist from Gujarat.

A Bhil woman is seen here, embellishing a wall. It is customary in the desert to decorate mud walls with mirrors and clay appliqué motifs, which are painted.

JOURNEYS: MERGING AND MARCHING ON

In this concluding chapter, we focus on the traditions of folk and tribal painting which have become popular, with special attention on the emerging trends.

POPULAR TRENDS

MADHUBANI[i]

Madhubani is the heartland of Mithila, the ancient country of the Maithilas, located in the Madhubani district of Bihar. Madhubani is derived from the words *madhu* and *ban* meaning the 'forest of honey', which implies the land of prosperity. Madhubani paintings were also recognized as '*Kulin*' art or the art of the pure castes. For a long time, Madhubani remained an inseparable part of the Maithila lifecycle, deeply associated with various rituals. It flourished as a household art, mainly as a part of the social customs and practices. The most prominent and pervasive elements of the visual idiom were the *sanskara* (tradition) and the *vrata*[ii] (fasts). The paintings were done as a part of the sacred rituals mainly associated with marriage. Madhubani folk art was practised by women from all stratas of society – the Brahmin, Kayastha or Harijan.

Apart from women painters, Brahmin priests from Mithila have also remained exponents of a particular form of Madhubani art, which has come to be recognized as an offshoot of tantric art. The Maithilas are a deeply religious society and are greatly influenced by Shiva, Vishnu and *shakti*, its energy and force being recognized in its various forms. Durga, the most powerful form of Parvati, a tantric goddess, has aroused the artistic sensibilities of the Madhubani painters. Visual expression of Madhubani tantric art is seen in the paintings of a Maithil Brahmin known as Lal Baba. As a matter of fact, popular

Facing page:
Peacock motif in the Madhubani style on a greeting card, paper, a reflection of the popular trend.

religion as manifested in the paintings by the womenfolk is corroborative of the existence of certain principles and theories, which are explained through *tantra*. The genesis of Madhubani art lies in tantric art. The pictorial forms are the human representations of *yantra*, the root of *tantra*. Various gods and goddesses personified in Madhubani folk art are each recognized by *yantra*, which is essentially a geometrical composition and represents a particular force, whose power of energy increases in proportion to the abstraction and precision of diagrams.

The colours which were traditionally used in this art form are also governed by certain underlying principles. Life is governed by five basic elements: *shiti* (earth), *jal* (water), *pavak* (fire), *gagan* (sky), and *samira* (air). These five basic sources of life are represented by five different colours. Earth is represented by the colour yellow, water is represented by white, red signifies fire, black symbolizes air and the vastness of the sky is indicated by blue. These five elements are also explained through three basic forms, namely, *trikon* (triangle), *golakar* (circle) and *chaukar* (square). The triangle can be drawn with the tip pointing towards the sky, *urdhamukha*, or the tip pointing downwards, *adhomukha*. Two triangles indicate fire and water respectively. The earth is represented by a square. The circumference of the circle denotes air, whereas the inner space of the circle means sky. The air and sky are interrelated. Fire and water, that is, heat and moisture are

also related. The forms emerge from *bindu*, the dot, which also represents Shiva and the goddess Shakti. Shiva is formless and visualizes his own forms in Shakti. When this occurs, a *mishra bindu* is formed.

Traditionally, the paintings were executed on the walls of three places in the home – the '*gosai ghar*' (room of the family deity), the '*kohbar ghar*' (the room for newly-wed couples), and the veranda outside the *kohbar ghar* used as a sitting room for visitors. *Kohbar* paintings symbolize fertility and creation.

Today, Madhubani painting has come a long way. While the ritual fervour may be lost in the commercial painting, the artist with a strong religious base continues to draw traditional forms as well as evolve new forms. Of late, painters have started using poster colours and Luxor fine-tipped pens with different inks. The introduction of fabric colours has provided a new opening for the transfer of Madhubani designs onto fabric for apparel as well as furnishing items.

BHIL PAINTINGS[III]

The Bhils and Bhilalas of Dhar and Jhabua in Madhya Pradesh and the Rathwas of Panchmahal and Baroda districts of Gujarat display characteristic ritual wall paintings created by traditional caste groups known as the Lakhindra. These paintings depict the story of creation and the myth thus depicted, centres around the tribal god Baba and his nephew,

Pithoro. Members of the Lakhindra caste group are chosen to execute these ritualistic paintings because of their natural aptitude for drawing. The main character of the Pithoro painting is the horse. Often, iron moulds of the horse in different sizes are used to draw the outline. After the painting is installed in the house, it is consecrated by the *bhopa* or priest-performer. The offerings aim for the well-being of the family and fertility.

Rendering of the paintings among the Bhils of Madhya Pradesh is simple and archaic. The main characters of Pithoro and Pithori are painted in white on cow dung plastered walls. The diagrammatic simplification of the painted forms in the Pithoro paintings of Madhya Pradesh bring them closer to the prehistoric rock paintings found in the region.

Pithoro paintings among the Rathwas of Panchmahal and Baroda districts of Gujarat are

Pithoro painting detail, Gujarat.

119

luxuriously colourful and ornamental. The rectangular boundary with a painting in the centre of the bottom border is marked as a gate where the marriage procession starts and moves further up. An important character in Pithoro paintings is '*chhinala*' – the shameless copulating couple. This element lends an erotic touch to the painted wall. Traditionally, when a Pithoro painting was installed on the wall of the house, each of the characters had to be illustrated according to the myth. However, the significant number of characters in the Pithoro paintings of Gujarat and Madhya Pradesh vary. Like many other wall paintings, these paintings are also now executed on paper and are being sold commercially out of their traditional context.

WARLI PAINTINGS

The name 'Warli painting', as mentioned earlier, has emerged from the tribe called Warlis, who live in the Thane district of Maharashtra. This district is situated in the north of Mumbai, and stretches up to the Gujarat border. The traditional drawings in Warli paintings are the *chowks*. Palaghat, the most significant Mother Goddess, is shown seated in the *chowk*. Various types of *chowks* feature in Warli paintings in different areas of the district. Palaghat, the deity, is drawn by making two triangles, with their tips meeting each other in the centre. These tips are cut and open, thus merging the triangles into one another. It is believed that this opening is for the flow of energy from one triangle to another. Interestingly, of these two triangles, the one facing downwards reflects female energies, indicating that the flow of the energies of women is directed downwards.

Since Warli tribals are agriculturists, Hariali Deva, the god of plants, also occupies a prominent place in the Warli pictograph. Other characters in the traditional Warli painting are Pancha Sirya Deva, the five-headed god, and the headless warrior, who is either standing or riding a horse. Pancha Sirya Deva is the archaic symbol of the cosmic cycle of life and death. Interestingly, a similar male deity is depicted in metallic images among the Bhils of Gujarat, where he is known as Panch Mukhi Deva.

Traditionally, menfolk painted the Warli pictographs or magical diagrams. In the late 1970s, married women or Savasinis started participating in the painting process together with the men. Warli women executed their fantasies by drawing circles around the primary motifs of Palaghat, who is represented by the triangles. Each drawing, whether of a human being, an animal, a plant or any other depicted form, emerges from two triangles with their tips facing each other. This practice of drawing triangles is accentuated by a splendid use of circles and dots. The selective imaginative use of triangles, circles and dots, only in white, on a muddy surface, gives a perfect magical vibrancy to the paintings done by the Warlis.

Rice paste was the traditional medium used

Facing page:
Warli painting showing village life, paper, Maharashtra.

for the drawings on mud walls. In modern times, Warli paintings have been brought out of the sanctity of the wall and transferred to paper. Initially, women were given paper and white poster colour to express their imagination as they chose. A sea change occurred in the recognition given to Warli paintings, when Jivya Soma Mase, a male painter, received a National Award for a large canvas in the early 1970s. This paved the way for the commercial marketing of Warli paintings. In contemporary Warli paintings, traditional *chowks* are slowly and steadily being taken over by other decorations. But even today, these paintings continue to be created at special occasions, such as the time of marriage in the humble homes of Warli tribals.

GOND PAINTINGS

Unlike the Warlis, the Gond tribals of district Mandla in Madhya Pradesh do not draw the boundaries of a painting. They place a dot, another dot and then a series of dots upwards, downwards and sideways, for the final image to appear. These dots, wherever required, are supplemented with elliptical, oval and triangular interceptions. The geometry of the drawing is bold as well as loud. The themes of the paintings are drawn from folktales and Gond mythology. For example, in one of the local Gond myths, it is said that Arjuna, one of the Pandavas, grew jealous of Krishna's friendly relations with young women in contrast to his own unrewarded passion for Subhadra. Arjuna retired to the forest in despair and painted his lovelorn state on the walls of his hut. Seeing the paintings by the desolate lover, Krishna took pity on him and facilitated a meeting between Arjuna and Subhadra.

The tradition of painting the walls of huts has continued since then. In recent times, Gond painters like Jangarh Singh Shyam have started painting on paper. Initially, the themes of their paintings were confined to scenes from forest magic, the world of ghosts and spirits, birds and animals, the sun and the moon, man and woman. Slowly, new themes like motor cars and trains have begun to be depicted. Each motif continues to be drawn with dots, triangles and chevrons. The boldness of these paintings in terms of colours renders them a class apart.

TATTOO PAINTINGS[IV]

Tattoo painting is the art of body decoration, which is exhibited on the forehead, chin, forearms, stomach, soles of the feet and ankles. Generally, among the folk communities, tattoos are restricted to simple motifs of three to five dots, which in the case of women are restricted to their names and, after marriage, the name of the husband. It is customary for women to have their bodies tattooed. The tribal communities, particularly the Pradhans of Mandla, Gonds of Chhattisgarh, Bastar in Madhya Pradesh and Orissa, Bhils of Rajasthan

and the Baigas, Banjaras, Kanwars, Kamars, Murias, Bhatras, Durlos, Kols, and Oraons of the Orissa and Madhya Pradesh states have tattooed decorations on their bodies. Men of the Naga tribe have their chests tattooed with designs of horns.

Tattoo motifs vary from tribe to tribe and region to region. Among the Pangia Khonds, a tribe from Orissa, Bhimal Pinnu, a local deity worshipped for fertility and rain, is depicted in the form of a tattoo on the faces of young girls. These tattoos are done if Bhimal appears in the dream of the young girl. Generally, tattooing is done in several stages while the girl is moving towards maturity, the first tattoo being etched when the girl is around the age of seven to eight years. The second tattooing is done around puberty, which publicly announces her reaching maturity, while the third stage is done just before marriage. If for any reason, the

parents of the girl are not able to tattoo her before her marriage, the custom is observed in the house of the in-laws. The Dewars, a sub-tribe of the Gonds, which is also considered to be a mixed tribe of Baigas and Kanwars, has professional women tattooists who are experts in the tattooing process.

The Dewarin women know the technique to prepare ink for tattooing by mixing soot with '*bhilawa*' oil. The prototypes of the motifs are drawn with an ink pen on the area where the motif is to be permanently tattooed. Then, with the help of a needle and ink, the motifs are pricked on the skin, and the design is created through a series of dots. The Baigas of the Mandla area prepare ink by burning the skins of cobras and mixing it in '*niggar*' seed oil.

The tattoo marks are considered to be a woman's wealth, which she carries with her

Gond paintings showing a woman catching a lion by its tail in a forest and an eagle carrying a child, paper, Madhya Pradesh.

even after death. These are seen as the ornaments of the spirits, which go to the Maha Prabhu (Shiva). The other reason given by the tribal communities for tattoo paintings is that the tattoos give extraordinary power to a person, enabling him or her to carry heavy weights. Tattoo marks on the soles of the feet protect them from getting hurt.

There are several motifs ranging from circles, lines, leaves, flowers, agricultural tools such as the sickle, mortal and pestle, and baskets. Elaborate tattooing also includes scenes from the Ramayana. The portion of the body, which requires additional strength, is tattooed with the specific image of the local deity among the Gond women. For example, the deity Ghora Dev is tattooed on the front thighs to give a person the strength of a horse. The image of Hanuman Dev is tattooed on the arms to make the upper arms strong. To represent Jhulna Devi, goddess of wings, the image of Bara Dev is tattooed on the breast. Bhimsen, the god of food, is tattooed on the back, generally to cure women, who have poor digestion.[v]

Today, the motifs and designs used in tattoo patterns are drawn on paper and sold as painted designs. Apart from the Dewarin women, Harijans of Madhubani, Bihar, also sell tattoo paintings. Some of the Dewarin tribes have gone a step ahead and show a woman with her whole body tattooed as an individual style of painting, a manifestation of the emerging trend of individualistic art.

In India, gambling has existed among all castes, classes and religions since ancient times. Along with the game of dice and other board games, the game of cards has been popular under the roadside tree as well as in the inner chambers of the noble courts since early times. Today, card parties after dinner or nights spent in gambling at the time of Diwali, are part of our lifestyle.

In days of yore, the game seemed to have been even more complicated and difficult to play. *Ganjifa* cards, which were the indigenous parallel to the present-day playing cards, are a visual delight and a card player's challenge.

A text dating to the mid-sixteenth century, called *Humayun Nama*, written by Begum Gulbadan, gives a detailed description of the game of cards as it was traditionally played. The Arabic word for playing cards is *waraq*, a word occurring in medieval texts, and literally means a leaf or page. A *waraq* contained 240 cards. *Ganjifa*, as the game was more often called, is derived from the word '*ganj*' which means wealth of money and grains. Thus, the term *ganjifa* was also indicative of the aim of gambling that formed the basis of the game.

The *Ain-i-Akbari* by Abul Fazl, another text belonging to the Mughal period, describes two packs of cards, which are different from each other – an ordinary pack for the commoners, and the one used by the sages, indicating that the game of cards was the means of entertainment as much for the ascetic as for the commoner. *Ganjifa* demanded players of high intellectual calibre because the simplest form of the game had eight suits. The present-day western-style pack of cards has only four suits: two of black and two of red. Imagine the alertness that must have been required to play a game of eight suits. Complex card games consisting of several suits of ten, twelve, sixteen, twenty-four, or thirty-two seem to have gone out of vogue. Emperor Akbar is believed to have simplified the game to contain eight suits. This is still a living game in parts of Orissa and Bengal. It is said that the simplified game of eight, ten and twelve suits became a very popular source of entertainment during the spread of imperial rule from the seventeenth century onward and penetrated the provincial courts and the elite strata throughout the country, except in the southern states of Tamil Nadu and Kerala.

As more and more people sought the *ganjifa* for entertainment, the designs and fashioning of the cards began to absorb elements from local art and culture. The game itself became complex, requiring a sharper memory. Consequently, several regional versions of these cards emerged, suiting different social strata, religions and attributes of mind. It is also recorded that several kings spent considerable time in inventing more and more complicated versions of *ganjifa*.

Ganjifa cards for the elite were made of ivory, tortoise-shell, mother-of-pearl, or of inlaid or enamelled precious metals. Wood,

Facing page:
Ganjifa playing cards, with incarnations of Vishnu, cardboard, Vishnupur, West Bengal, mid-20th century.

engraved brass discs, leather, silver, sandalwood and fish seals are also reported to have been used as the materials for the *ganjifa* cards. Palm-leaf, starched cotton fabric or paper are materials used even today. The process of making the *ganjifa* cards depends on the base material. However, irrespective of the material used, various suits of each pack were and continue to be distinguished by the illustrations on them. These cards were thematically designed in two main styles based on the Muslim and Hindu religion. They usually came in two sizes of five-centimetre diameter and ten-centimetre diameter.

The cards in the Muslim style had illustrations suiting the nomenclature of the court. For example, the twelve-suited *ganjifa* pack of the court of Akbar had six suits, each of the powerful ones known as Bishbar and six suits of the weak ones known as Kambar. They were represented by various images of horses, elephants, serpents, men or soldiers, ladies, forts, treasures, battleships, divinities, demons and jungles. Since each character was divided into the trio of king, minister and suit sign, the cards had interesting stylized illustrations of each.

Ashwapati, known as the king of Dilli (present Delhi) was represented on horseback, with an umbrella, while his minister was shown seated on a horse. The suit sign was a horse. Gajapati or the lord of elephants was said to represent the king of Orissa, while Narpati was the king of Bijapur in the Deccan. Interestingly, the cards with military characters representing the realistic domain were considered to be more powerful than the characters from Hindu and Muslim mythology. For example, Surapati was the representation of Indra, the king of Hindu gods. Banpati was represented by a tiger with other animals and Ahipati was a large snake riding on a dragon, representing the netherworld. All these deities were considered to be less powerful than the kings of neighbouring places represented in the cards.

The less complicated characters of the eight-suited *ganjifa* pack had eight king characters such as 'Padish-i-zari-i-surkh', the king of the gold coin, dispensing money from his throne, or the 'Padishah-i-barat', the king of the documents, inspecting papers on his throne. Other kings represented in the cards were of merchandise, yaks, harps, swords, slaves, and so on. These cards, used by the people of the court, were painted on ivory by the court artists and were most lavishly decorated.

The most popular theme for the Hindu version of the *ganjifa* was the Dasavatar, the ten incarnations of Lord Vishnu. The *matsya* or the fish avatar (incarnation), right up to the avatar that is yet to come, the *kalki* avatar, are represented both in their animal and anthropomorphic forms. Two cards of the king with his ministers, completes the set.

Similar to the Mughal pattern, in this pack too, the first suits are weak, while the last five are strong. Interestingly, the motifs and colours for the lead card for night and day are different. The motif for the day is that of Krishna, an incarnation of Lord Vishnu or his brother, Balaram, considered by some schools of thought to be yet another incarnation of Lord Vishnu himself. The lead card for the game, when played at night is Vishnu's incarnation as Rama. The colours and the representations for each of the incarnations are specific, for instance, the incarnation where Vishnu appears as a dwarf is represented by a blue water jug, while the one in which he appears as a fish is painted in black. With an increase in the number of suits, more deities were added to the card game. The first ones to be included were the elephant god Ganesha and his brother Kartikeya. When even larger packs were to be designed, Lord Brahma the Creator, Shiva the Destroyer and Vishnu the Protector are followed with images of all the other gods in Hindu mythology, such as Yama, the god of death, Indra the king of heaven, and others.

The other illustrative expressions from Hindu mythology in *ganjifa* cards have themes from the Ramayana. The hero Rama and the anti-hero Ravana form the strong and weak sets in this card game based on the Ramayana. A few other illustrated diversions in the Hindu tradition are the tantric *ganjifa* cards, the Navagraha or the nine planets depicted on the cards and those based on the zodiac signs.

In many parts of rural Andhra Pradesh, Karnataka, Rajasthan, Tamil Nadu and Orissa, *ganjifa* cards are still being made and played with. In Orissa, there is a belief that playing the cards based on the incarnations of Lord Vishnu pleases the deity, but that could be just another excuse for gambling.

The standard playing cards of India fall under two categories: the Mughal *Ganjifa* (96-card set) and the Dasavtar *Ganjifa* (120-card set). *Ganjifa* cards are handmade, hand-painted and lacquered in several centres in Andhra Pradesh, Orissa, Bishnupur (West Bengal) and Sawantwadi (Maharashtra) as collectors' items as well as for play. Since *ganjifa* is a game of cards and carries with it the thrill of gambling, it has always been tremendously popular as a game. However, the cards are more valued for the colourful images that decorate them.

MANDANA

The art of creating designs on the floor has been an expression of joy and celebration on

mandana is *rangoli* in Maharashtra, *kolam* in Kerala, *alpana* in West Bengal, *aripan* in Bihar, *thapna* in Uttaranchal, *chowk purna* or *sona rakhana* in Uttar Pradesh and *sathia* in Gujarat.

The ground is prepared with cow dung mixed with *rati*, a local clay, and red ochre. Lime or chalk powder is used for making the motif. The brush is almost absent in *mandana* art. The tools employed for making the designs are a piece of cotton or a tuft of hair. These work as an ink filter in a fountain pen. The third finger in which this tuft is held, acts as a nib. Sometimes a rudimentary brush made out of a date stick is used for drawing. Village women in the Sawai Madhopur area of Rajasthan possess a spontaneous skill for developing designs of perfect symmetry and accuracy. Wherever required, circles or triangles are drawn by using a thread. Many a time, the arm becomes the measure of scale.

The architectural motifs in *mandana* art are made by first plotting the points. A set of three points may be plotted to make an equilateral triangle. The receding patterns may be drawn by plotting ten, eight, six, four or two points in descending order. If the design is asymmetrical, an odd number of points such as nine, seven, five, or three may be plotted.

Drawings of circles or polygons may contain many variations of design in the space within, with each part being likened to a single point in the centre or a set of three points. Thus, *mandana* art has an almost limitless quality of

festive occasions and as part of the daily routine in Indian homes, down the ages. These designs are believed to bring harmony to a home. The art is known as '*mandana*' in parts of Rajasthan and Madhya Pradesh, and consists of geometrical designs drawn on mud floors and walls as part of ritual and festive practices. These geometrical designs originate from eastern Rajasthan, particularly in the Bundi and Jhalawar areas of Rajasthan and Bundelkhand, and the Gwalior and Nimar regions of Madhya Pradesh. The equivalent of

extension. The *mandanas* are surrounded by smaller motifs, which often have *paglya* or footprints, which signify the doorway to the drawing, which in turn leads the way to the deities. The interlocked stripes or the pathways denote the total design laid on the floor.

HENNA PAINTING

Women in Rajasthan and Gwalior were traditionally skilled in drawing *mehndi* (henna) designs on the palm. In the traditional parlance of folk paintings, the art of making designs on the palm and the feet may not be considered as a style of folk drawing. But looking closely at the *mehndi* designs, we find that this art is an outgrowth of *mandana* art, particularly in Rajasthan and Madhya Pradesh. Women apply the henna paste in a very concentrated form on the palms and the feet with the thumb and index finger, as in *mandana*. The intricacy and fineness of the designs, of course, vary from artist to artist.

The art of henna design has now permeated into modern fashion, and is so popular that commercial *mehndi* artists are found sitting in the vicinity of various markets, temples and fairs. Today, plastic cones or sticks are used to draw the designs.

In today's scenario, the global buyer recognizes the intrinsic value of tribal and folk paintings and art forms, and wants to support their continuity. This has led to the commercial development of tribal and folk art by the use of materials and forms suitable for the market. An interesting phenomenon that can be observed is the merging and blending of two or more tribal and folk traditions in the commercial rendition of the paintings. Several development corporations such as Trifed (Tribal Cooperative Marketing Development Federation of India Limited) are involved in promoting tribal art through handmade greeting cards, bookmarks and other items. Several of the greeting cards blend images of Gond, Bhil and Warli traditions. The Muria

Intricate henna designs on a woman's palms and fingers, Rajasthan.

tribals from Chhattisgarh depict the traditional *ghotul* – the dormitory of the youth and the activities carried on around the *ghotul*. It is customary among the Gond tribals to have group dances performed in a circle to the rhythmic beat of the drum. These dances are now visually depicted by the Muria artist in the same manner as the Warli dance is depicted in Warli painting.

JOURNEYS

SANTOKHBA, THE FOLK ARTIST

As the tribal artists grow in recognition, some are showing tremendous energy to draw and paint, even when elderly. Santokhba, a painter from Gujarat, ventured into painting the Mahabharata on a kilometre-long canvas. This unique canvas is in the collection of the Indira Gandhi National Centre for the Arts in New Delhi. Santokhba has given this powerful theme, which is a recurring one in many folk paintings, a sense of space through a variety of trees, some of them mythological, and plenty with flowers, foliage and birds.

In this unique canvas, Santokhba has been creative in her depiction, co-relating mythological themes with the world around her. Her powerful strokes are not limited to the canvas as she has also done illustrations for children's literature based on the Mahabharata. Instead of the traditional harmonizing of earthy colours like Indian red or burnt sienna with

yellow ochre, which are used in most folk art of Saurashtra and Rajasthan, Santokhba prefers bright turquoise blue, red and yellow ochre and deep green, with each motif prominently outlined in black. However, the colour arrangement of each panel is not synchronized but radically varies, as if to give power to the subject. For example, in the introductory panel, where the sage Veda Vyasa is depicted dictating the invocatory *shlokas* to Lord Ganesha, one can see a bright aura around Vyasa and none around Ganesha. She indicates the importance of the scene with her selection of colour.

Santokhba derives inspiration from her surroundings and then superimposes it on her scroll. Another highlight of the scroll is the court of Satyapal. Santokhba's maturity is evident in the multi-dimensional composition of the scene. The ministers at the court sit in two rows, facing each other. She has depicted one row in profile, bringing out their headgear and seats. No intricate detail is left out. The sun and the moon painted on a white background at the top of this panel are interesting elements. The sun has a smiling face and the crescent moon has half-closed, meditative eyes that give the viewer a soothing celestial effect. War scenes have no evidence of bloodshed among the hordes of marching troops, elephants, chariots and horses, the only sign of blood being the red rings painted on the tips of arrows. Santokhba contemplatively explains this facet of her art: 'Enough blood has been spilt in this world, so I do not want to further the sorrow by the sight of blood on my canvas.'

INSPIRATIONS

The number of tribal and folk painters who paint, exhibit and sell their work alongside other contemporary painters is on the increase each day. Many folk and tribal painters are now holding group shows in reputed art galleries. A beginning in this direction was made by artist Jamini Ray and an elaborate type of art inspired by folk art started to emerge in the work and style of other artists too. Today, several renowned artists, such as Arpana Caur, derive their inspiration from folk and tribal art – which is now nationally and internationally recognized – and blend the age-old themes of this art into their work in a vibrant fusion.

Tribal painting on greeting card, paper, Madhya Pradesh.

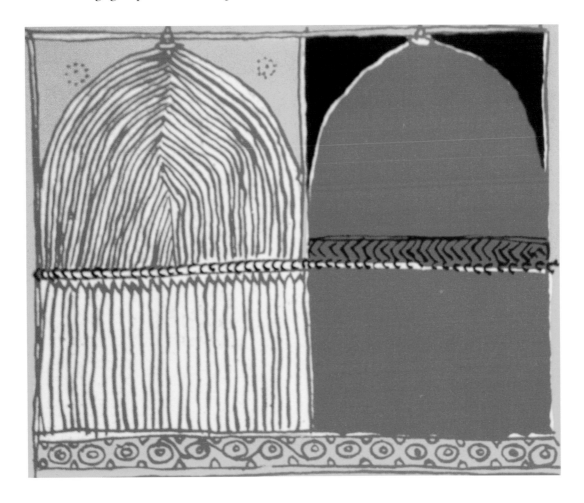

ACKNOWLEDGEMENTS

A visual encyclopaedia for apprising people of various styles of tribal and folk painting on different surfaces, the National Handicrafts and Handlooms Museum (NHHM) is located at Pragati Maidan, New Delhi. Village Complex, the open air museum displaying the vernacular architectural forms from various regions, features village shrines, verandas, walls and galleries that project different styles of tribal and folk paintings. These painted forms are further complemented by a demonstration of their skills by craftspersons every month and the collections in the stores. My research for this monograph is mainly based on my observations and research of the projection of tribal and folk paintings in NHHM, Ministry of Textiles, and during the fieldwork conducted in various parts of the country. I gratefully acknowledge the support of the Senior Director and staff of the NHHM. I am also indebted to all the tribal and folk painters who have perpetuated the art of painting and brought these skills to a recognized forum.

PHOTO CREDITS

Facing page: Mural painting of Nataraja, the god of dance, in the dancing posture of Lord Shiva. This avatar is the main deity in the famous temple at Chidambaram, south India.

BIBLIOGRAPHY

Agarwal, D.P. and J.S. Kharakwal. (2002), *South Asian Prehistory*, New Delhi: Aryan Books International.

Agrawal, O.P. and R. Pathak. (2001), *Examination and Conservation of Wall Paintings: A Manual*, New Delhi: Sundeep Prakashan.

Appasamy, J. (1980), *Tanjavur Painting of the Maratha Period*, New Delhi: Abhinav Publications.

Appasamy, J. (1980), *Indian Glass Painting*, New Delhi: ICCR.

Appasamy, J. (1985), *The Critical Vision, Selected Writings*, New Delhi: Lalit Kala Akademi.

Archer, Mildred. (1977), *Indian Popular Paintings*, London: Her Majesty's stationery office.

Archer, Mildred. (1992), *Company Paintings: Indian Paintings of the British Period*, Ahmedabad: Mapin Publishing Pvt. Ltd.

Archer, W.G. (1971), *Kalighat Paintings*, London: Her Majesty's stationery office.

Barnes, R., Stevan Cohen and Rosemary Crill. (2002), *Trade, Temple and Court, Indian Textiles from the Tapi Collection*, Mumbai: India Book House.

Bhatt, J. (1991), 'Sanja: A Traditional Art Form', *India* magazine 11, no. 12, pp.20–31, Bombay.

Bhattacharya, A.K.(1995), *A Pageant of Indian Culture; Arts and Archaeology*, 2 Volumes, New Delhi: Abhinav Publications.

Dalmia, Yashodhara (1988), *The Painted World of Warlis*, New Delhi: Lalit Kala Akademi.

Das, J.P. (1982), *Puri Paintings*, New Delhi: Arnold Heinemann.

Das, J.P. (1996), *The Painted Icons, Wall Paintings of the Sauras of South Orissa*, New Delhi: Harman Publishing House.

Das, J.P. and J. Williams (1991), *Palm Leaf Miniatures, The Art of Raghunath Prusti of Orissa*, New Delhi: Abhinav Publications.

Elwin, Verrier. (1951), *Tribal Art of Middle India*, London: Oxford University Press.

Fischer, E. and Dinanath Pathy. (1996), *Murals for Goddesses and Gods, The Tradition of Oshakothi Ritual Paintings in Orissa*, New Delhi: IGNCA.

Gupta, C.S. (1986), 'Madhubani – The Religious Folk Idiom' in the *Times of India*, New Delhi, 31 January.

Islam, Mazhrul. (1985), *Folklore: The Pulse of the People of India*, New Delhi, Concept Publications.

Jackson, David and Janice Jackson. (1988), *Tibetan Thangka Paintings Methods and Materials*, London: Serindia Publications.

Jain, J. (1984), *Painted Myths of Creation: Art and Ritual of an Indian Tribe*, New Delhi: Lalit Kala Akademi.

Jain J. (ed.) (1998), *Other Masters*, New Delhi: Crafts Museum and HHEC.

Jain, J. (1999), *Kalighat Painting, Images from a Changing India*, Ahmedabad: Mapin Publishing Pvt. Ltd.

Jayakar, Pupul. (1980), *Earthen Drum*, New Delhi: National Museum.

Kang, K.S. (1985), *Wall Paintings of Punjab and Haryana*, Delhi: Atma Ram and Sons.

Knizkova, Hana. (1975), *The Drawings of Kalighat Style*, Prague: Naprstek Museum Publishing.

Lazaro, Desmond Peter. (2005), *The Pichhvai Painting Tradition of Rajasthan,* Ahmedabad: Mapin Publishing Pvt. Ltd.

Leydon, R.V. (1982), *Ganjifa:* The Playing Cards of India, London Victoria and Albert Museum.

Mandal, H. and Sunit Mukherjee, *et al.* (2002), *India: An Illustrated Atlas of the Tribal World*, Calcutta: ASI.

Majumdar, M.R. (1968), *Gujarat's Art Heritage*, University of Bombay.

Mathpal, Y. (1984), *Prehistoric Rock Paintings of Bhimbetka, Central India*, New Delhi: Abhinav Publications.

Mathpal, Y. (1998), *Rock Art in Kerala*, New Delhi: IGNCA.

Mishra, U.C. (1989), *Tribal Paintings and Sculptures*, Delhi: B.R. Publications.

Neumayer, E. (1983), *Prehistoric Indian Rock Paintings*, New Delhi: Oxford University Press.

Pal, M.K. (1978), *Crafts and Craftsmen in Traditional India*, New Delhi: Kanak Publications.

Prasad, A.K. (Col.). (2004), *Important Discoveries of Prehistoric Rock Paintings in Purattatva 34*, pp.68-90 New Delhi: Indian Archaeological Society .

Qaiser, A.J. (1996), *Art and Culture Endeavours in Interpretation*, New Delhi: Abhinav Publications.

Ray, Bidut Lata. (1998), *Jagannatha Cult: Origin, Rituals, Festivals, Religion and Philosophy*, Delhi: Kant Publications.

Saksena, J. (1985), *Mandana: A Folk Art of Rajasthan*, New Delhi: Crafts Museum.

Saxena, Madhu. (2004), *Bundelkhand Paintings: Orchha, Chhatarpur and Gwalior*, Delhi: Sharda Publishing House.

Shashi, M. (1982), 'Rock paintings and other antiquities of prehistoric and later times', Memoirs of the Archeological Survey of India, no.24.

Shastri, Archana. (n.d.), *Language of Symbol*, New Delhi: Crafts Council of India.

Sivaramamurti, C. (1994), *South Indian Paintings,* National Museum, New Delhi: National Museum.

Skeleton, Robert. (1973), *Rajasthani Temple Hanging of the Krishna Cult*, New York: The American Federation of Art.

Skeleton, R. and M. Francis, (1979), *Arts of Bengal*, pp.34-56. London: V&A.

Smita, C. (1977), 'Wall Paintings in a Gujarati Village' in *Folklore*, vol. 18, no.11, pp.352–58.

Sundara, A. (1984), 'Some Select Rock Paintings from North Karnataka', *Rock Art of India* (ed. K.K. Chakravarty), pp.137-48. New Delhi: Moti Lal Banarasi Das

Traditional Paintings : Old and New, (1989) New Delhi: Lalit Kala Akademi (exhibition catalogue).

Vardarajan, L. (1982), *South Indian Traditions of Kalamkari*, Ahmedabad: National Institute of Design.

Verma, Vimla. (1987), *Uttar Pradesh Ki Lok Kala, Bhoomi aur Bhitti Alankaran*, Delhi: Jai Shri Prakashan.

ENDNOTES

THE BEGINNING

i   *Radio carbon dates from Mesolithic deposits of Bhimbetka and other sites in central India range from 8000 BP to 3000 BP; Y. Mathpal, 1984: 220. BP here, stands for 'Before Present'.*

ii   *A.K. Prasad, 2004: 68–90.*

iii   *Folk and tribal art, being simple and direct with minimum application of colour, are closely compared to rock art; Y. Mathpal, 1984: 218.*

iv   *Y. Mathpal, 1984: 205.*

v   *Red ochre known as* geru *is a red mineral substance for colouring; a partially decomposed haematite (iron peroxide).*

vi   *D.P. Agrawal and J.S. Kharakwal, 2002: 126–156.*

vii   *Y. Mathpal, 1998: 22–34.*

viii   *Y. Mathpal, 1998: 41–44.*

ix   *Y. Mathpal, 1998: 51.*

x   *A. Sundara, 1984: 137–148.*

xi   *Y. Mathpal, 1984: 217.*

xii   *V. Elwin, 1951: 170.*

xiii   *V. Elwin, 1951: 90.*

xiv   *J. Appasamy, 1985: 8.*

xv   *Kapila Vatsyayan explains that the diachronic interpretation has three stages. First, is the modern interpretation of traditional art forms, the second is moving back in time to the rock art stage, and the third is constructing a conceptual framework by juxtaposing visual text with the cultural context (Y. Mathpal, 1998: x).*

xvi   *P. Jayakar, 1980.*

STYLES AND SURFACES: A BRIEF HISTORY

i   *Y. Mathpal, 1984.*

ii   *H. Mandal, 2002: 105–106.*

iii   *H. Mandal, 2002: III.*

iv   *Pando and Satnami tribes are skilled in tattoo or body paintings. Dhankul* puja *and painted cenotaphs are traditional paintings of Bastar.*

v   *M.K. Pal, 1978: pl. I, II, III.*

vi   *P. Jayakar, 1980: 88.*

vii   *J. Appasamy, 1985: 82.*

viii   *A.J. Qaisar, 1996: 153.*

ix   *Mineral pigments are made from rocks and stones, including semi-precious stones such as malachite for green and lapis lazuli for blue. Earth colours are obtained from earth surface deposits: examples are* ramraj *(yellow ochre) and* geru *(red ochre). Organic colours are made from plants, animals or insects. Pigments made by chemical process are alchemical colours: examples are* sindur *(vermillion),* asmani *(smalt). D.P. Lazaro, 2005: 62.*

x   *M.R. Majmudar, 1968.*

xi   *Marg, 1983: 61.*

xii   *E. Fischer and D. Pathy, 1996.*

xiii   *J. Jain, 1984.*

xiv   *I had seen these paintings during a field visit to the area in 1976.*

xv   *C. Smita, 1977: 352–358, 365.*

xvi   *A.K. Bhattacharya, 1995: 43–44.*

xvii   *A.K. Bhattacharya, 1995: 48–49.*

xviii   *R. Skelton, 1979.*

xix   *R. Barnes, 2001.*

xx   *These are techniques in which cloth is dipped in a mordant solution or a space is blocked by putting a resist. If such a process is done with a pen, it is a painting.*

xxi   *P. Jayakar, 1981.*

xxii   *P. Jayakar, 1981.*

xxiii   *R. Skeleton, 1979:3 8.*

xxiv   *J. Jain, 1999.*

MANIFESTATIONS OF PAINTED FORMS

i   *Based on conversations with the painters from Orissa.*

ii   *M. Islam, 1985.*

iii   *C. Smita, 1977: 356.*

iv   *C. Smita, 1977: 353.*

v   *P. Jayakar, 1980.*

vi   *J. Saksena, 1985.*

vii   *Information gathered from Madhubani artist.*

viii   *D. Jackson and J. Jackson, 1988: 82.*

ix   *Y. Mathpal, 1998.*

x   *D.P. Lazaro, 2005: 64.*

xi   *D. Jackson and J. Jackson, 1988: 79.*

xii   *D.P. Lazaro, 2005: 62.*

IDENTITIES

i   *J. Appasamy, 1980: 13.*

ii   *D.P. Lazaro, 2005: pp. 14–44.*

iii   *Govardhan is a hillock in Govardhan area, near Mathura in Uttar Pradesh.*

iv   *R. Skelton, 1973.*

v   *J.P. Das, 1982.*

vi   *B.L. Ray, 1998: 17.*

vii   *J.P. Das, 1982.*

viii   *J. Appasamy, 1980: 27.*

ix   *J. Appasamy, 1980: 24.*

x   *J. Jain, 1999.*

xi   *H. Knizkova, 1975: 7.*

xii   *J. Jain, 1999.*

xiii   *Based on personal interview with Chandaraya Nakkash.*

xiv   *Traditional painting, 1989.*

xv   *Painting done by the National Awardee Vijay Joshi of Shahpura, Bhilwara district, Rajasthan.*

xvi   *L. Vardarajan, 1982.*

xvii   *M. Archer, 1978: 173–174.*

xviii   *V. Verma, 1987: 15.*

xix   *U.C. Mishra, 1989: 5.*

xx   *U.C. Mishra, 1989: 12.*

xxi   *J. Bhatt, 1991, p. 23.*

xxii   *J. Bhatt, 1991, p. 28*

xxiii   *E. Fischer and D. Pathy, 1996.*

xxiv   *E. Fischer and D. Pathy, 1996: 87.*

xxv   *E. Fischer and D. Pathy, 1996: 21–22.*

xxvi   *E. Fischer and D. Pathy, 1996: 27–41.*

xxvii   *D. Pathy, 1996.*

xxviii   *A. Shastri, n.d..*

xxix   *J.P. Das and J. Williams, 1991.*

JOURNEYS: MERGING AND MARCHING ON

i   *C.S. Gupta, 1986.*

ii   *Sanskaras are the various domestic ceremonies or rites which a household is bound to perform for the continuity of the life energy cycle. Ceremonies like upanayana (sacred thread), mundan (first haircut), marriage, birth etc. Vratas are the religious acts of devotion observed on certain days in the year associated with the deities or seasons.*

iii   *J. Jain, 1984.*

iv   *V. Elwin, 1951.*

v   *U. C. Mishra, 1989.*

vi   *R.V. Leydon, 1982.*